MACRAMÉ:
THE ART OF
CREATIVE KNOTTING

Small pieces of macramé were knotted of French cotton embroidery yarns and then assembled on a woven background to make a collage. Some stitchery and beads were used to enrich the composition.

MACRAMÉ:
THE ART OF
CREATIVE KNOTTING

Virginia I. Harvey

Van Nostrand Reinhold Company
New York   Cincinnati   London   Toronto   Melbourne

Van Nostrand Reinhold Company Regional Offices:
New York   Cincinnati   Chicago   Millbrae   Dallas

Van Nostrand Reinhold Company International Offices:
London   Toronto   Melbourne

Designed by Emilio Squeglio.
Published by Van Nostrand Reinhold Company, a Division of Litton Educational Publish-
ing, Inc., 450 West 33rd Street, New York, N. Y. 10001.
Published simultaneously in Canada by Van Nostrand Reinhold Ltd.

16   15   14   13

CONTENTS

Acknowledgments and Introduction   6

1. Macramé, Past and Present   9
2. Tools   33
3. Materials for Macramé   39
4. Preparation for Knotting   49
5. Learning the Basic Knots   55
6. Other Knots   69
7. Design and Color in Macramé   81
8. Mounting, Shaping, and Finishing   105
9. Planning a Knotting Project   121

List of Suppliers   126
Bibliography   127
Glossary and Index of Knots   128

ACKNOWLEDGMENTS

It is not possible to mention all of the people who have helped in the preparation of this book. Complete strangers have written long letters in answer to questions. People in the business world have taken time from busy schedules to help me solve a problem. Continual association with creative people tends to mold and shape your ideas and standards.

It was Jacqueline Enthoven who urged me to write a book about macramé, and she advised and helped me continuously during the work. Knowing that a book about this subject would rely heavily on photography, I was also influenced by the fact that it was possible to have William Eng take the photographs. I think they speak for themselves. Not only does he take superb photographs of difficult subjects, but he is also a unique and wonderful person to work with. In the four color plates, the yarns and the fabrics were reproduced exactly by the Dudley, Hardin, and Yang firm.

Many of the illustrations were knotted by Charles Frisbie, who was known as "Mr. Macramé" in the Pacific Northwest. Since he taught the technique and made countless pieces of macramé, it is regrettable that he did not live to see this publication. His wife, Betsy Frisbie Ekvall, was most helpful in locating pieces of his knotting and in encouraging me with the work.

For the tedious job of preparing the final inked drawings, I am most grateful to Virginia Von Phul. In the final rush to meet the deadline, she was helped by Jon Pokela and by my younger son, Russell. Credit for typing most of the manuscript must be given to Penelope Helms.

In a book that is full of directions, diagrams, and photographs, the design, sequence, and lay-out of the material is very important. Both the editor, Nancy C. Newman, who suggested some rearrangement of the text and called my attention to errors, and Emilio Squeglio, who designed the book, have my deep appreciation for their skillful work.

Many of my associates at the University of Washington have learned to knot, and I have profited by their experiences. Four of us, Marrietta Ward, Gilda Van Norman, Harriet Marshall, and I, learned together during lunch-hour sessions. We searched for publications on the subject, tried different materials, and made many useful things for ourselves and our families.

During the period of intense work on the manuscript, I called my husband my "keeper." Although he has a full schedule of his own, he shouldered many of my responsibilities. Without his help and understanding, and the cooperation and interest of our two sons, William Jr. and Russell, it would not have been possible to write the book.

Virginia Isham Harvey

INTRODUCTION

"I could never do that! It's much too complicated." This is the reaction I have heard from almost everyone who sees a piece of macramé or encounters someone working on a knotted piece. Indeed, it does look complicated; it is deceptive, however. I learned the technique by following the diagrams in a French book, and I can't read French. After trying several of the combinations in the book, I suddenly realized that most of the knotting is done with two simple knots that I had tied all my life. I could hardly believe it. It is just a matter of combining these knots into patterns that makes it become macramé. I am sure that when people pick up this book and leaf through it, they too will think macramé is very difficult. I wish the title could have read, "Honestly, it's easy!" Even then I doubt if the reader would believe it until he had tried it.

This book is meant to serve as a springboard for the knotter who wishes to design his own work, as well as a guide for the craftsman who prefers to work from a pattern. Those who have a practical turn of mind can make many handsome and very serviceable objects with macramé. It offers a very versatile medium to artists and designers who are more concerned with creating form and texture.

There is something satisfying about the act of tying and creating with knots. It is fun to treat the craft as a playful thing. After you have learned the knots, take a ball of string and play with the material, thinking only of texture and pattern and contrasts, with no idea of a purpose for the piece. It is good for us occasionally to turn off the practical and turn on the playful.

After learning the knots and gaining experience by knotting a few pieces, it should be possible to "read" a knotted object and tell how it was knotted. The chapter on design will show you how the knots fit together to form pattern and serve as a reference and inspiration for designing your own patterns.

Unfortunately there is confusion in the names that have been used for the knots. The same knot may be known by a different name in each book you read. I have tried to use simple, graphic terms that require no specialized knowledge to understand them. A glossary of terms is included at the back of the book as a further aid.

The drawings that illustrate the knots and patterns are diagrams that are not always an exact reproduction of the knotting as it will appear. When it was necessary to decide between a realistic rendering and a graphic illustration of how the knot was made, the latter was always chosen.

Before the text was started, my husband and I took "The Turtle" (our camper mounted on a pick-up truck) and traveled across the United States. I was searching for people who were knotting, as well as for historical and contemporary examples of macramé. There were many disappointments because it was seldom that I found very much information, and there were many lengthy explanations before others understood what I was seeking. However, I found a few good historical pieces, which are shown in Chapter One, and many other examples were located through correspondence.

My knotting base and cords went with us on the trip, and there is a trail of people from Seattle to Bangor, Maine to San Francisco and back to Seattle who will recognize macramé when they see it. Most of the examples that were photographed for Chapter Seven were knotted en route. Many other pieces used for illustrations were knotted by me, and they can be identified because neither the source of the knotting nor the knotter is mentioned in the caption of the illustration.

I have made an effort to use the work of other craftsmen as examples when a suitable piece could be found. But after many months of macramé-hunting and following many clues, I have decided that macramé could almost be classed as a dying technique. A few people are knotting and some recognize it as something they saw as children, but the majority of the people I met had neither seen it nor heard of it. It is a craft that should not be lost, so if this book serves to keep it alive, the effort of writing it will have been worth-while.

Virginia Isham Harvey

FIGURE 1-1

Figures of men and women are alternated in this seventeenth-century macramé lace from Italy. (Courtesy of the Art Institute of Chicago)

1

MACRAMÉ, PAST AND PRESENT

Knotting is an art so old that there is no record of its beginnings. We can only guess, but it seems logical that man would have used a knot when he needed to attach two vines together. This may have been his first step toward forming a textile, preceding both spinning and weaving. The earliest knotted textiles that have survived are game bags and nets used for catching wild beasts. These are at the Kircheriano Museum in Rome, Italy.

As civilization advanced and man's ingenuity led to more complex designs, knotting was used for decorative as well as utilitarian purposes. Fringes on some of the costumes of Babylonian and Assyrian sculptures appear to include both knotting and plaiting. The Arabic world was known for elaborate knotted fringes, and the term "macramé" is probably derived from an Arabic word meaning, literally, an object to protect or defend something. It was used in Arabic literature for a kerchief or shawl to protect the head. As the word found its way into the Italian language, it came to mean a towel or the material from which towels are made. Eventually macramé was identified with the knotted fringe on a towel, and it is now used to mean the knotting itself, regardless of where it is found. After 1500 macramé developed into its present form simultaneously with needle-made lace and bobbin lace, mostly in Italy and Spain.

Early macramé was knotted from the unwoven ends of a fabric, thus forming a lacy patterned finish instead of an abrupt ending such as a hem. Since the yarns forming the fabric were fine, the knotting was also fine, and it was called macramé lace. Later the lace was also made separately and attached as a trimming to the edge of household linens or garments. These laces frequently included figures of men and women in their design (Fig. 1-1).

Many of the designs of macramé have an Arab-Moresque character, like its name. Ada Treves Segre of Rehovot, Israel, wrote in a letter:

Born in Italy, I was taught macramé when a little girl (I am now over ninety) by my grandmother; she thought it had been brought by the Moors into Spain on their invasion of that country. It was originally meant for fringes to enrich towels, especially employing some of the bottom of the tissue and enriching it by knotting a few threads together. In this form it appeared later in Italy, especially at the seaside where fishermen's wives, used to knotting nets, worked macramé, but in a rather plain way.

My older sister, during her wedding trip in Spain, was surprised and enthralled at seeing in the Alhambra Museum some macramé works which in richness of design and purity of style greatly differed from what she had ever

A lace-maker's sample made to record a pattern. 4½ by 5½ inches. (Courtesy of Ada Treves Segre)

FIGURE 1-2

seen in Italy. Of one of the best patterns, she copied the enclosed lace. (Fig. 1-2)

The popularity of macramé has waxed and waned according to the dictates of fashion. Mrs. Palliser, in her volume on the history of lace, mentions a rediscovery of the technique in the mid-nineteenth century in Italy, where it was used for church

Nineteenth-century parasol with macramé lace trimming. (From *Sylvia's Book of Macramé Lace*)

FIGURE 1-3

Right. Linen. 15 inches long. (Courtesy of the Smithsonian Institution)

FIGURE 1-4

Nineteenth-century cravat with macramé lace trimming. (From *Sylvia's Book of Macramé Lace*)

purposes, linens, and fine fashion trimmings (Figs. 1-3 and 1-4). In addition to its domestic uses, macramé was exported to South America and California. The technique also appears in other European countries during the last half of the nineteenth century. Books on macramé were published in both England and France. Since decorative styles favored elaborate trimmings at that time, these books included illustrations of many knotted fringes (Figs. 1-5 and 1-6) and other passementerie. Most of the trimmings were made of heavier yarns than the older macramé laces, and they were usually referred to simply as macramé.

Regardless of the fashion trends, there seems to have been a continuous interest in macramé in the Mediterranean area. Schools and convents taught it to young children of both sexes. Mrs. Palliser says:

Right. Ivory cotton. Knotted by Anna Parker. (Courtesy of the Philadelphia Museum of Art. Photograph by A. J. Wyatt, Staff Photographer)

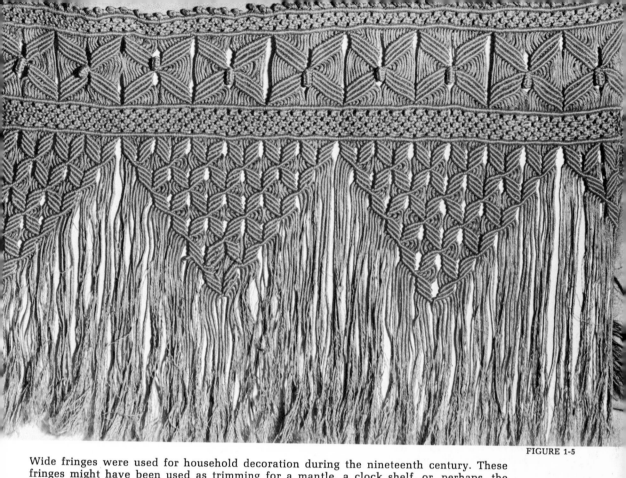

FIGURE 1-5

Wide fringes were used for household decoration during the nineteenth century. These fringes might have been used as trimming for a mantle, a clock shelf, or, perhaps, the edge of window drapery.

FIGURE 1-6

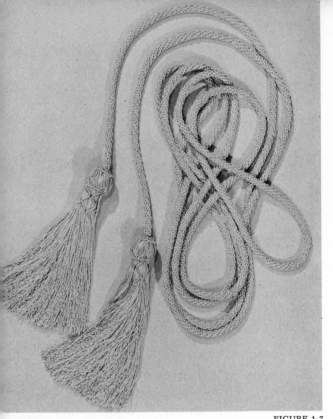

FIGURE 1-7

A cincture cord for a priest's robe. The cord is crocheted; macramé decorates the tassels. Knotted with dark yellow rayon yarn by Sister Catherine Mary, S.N.J.M.

"It was carried to great perfection at Chiavari and the Albergo de' Poveri at Genoa." Nuns are still knotting the trimmings for religious garments (Fig. 1-7) and linens for the Church.

Knotting in some form is native to most cultures, but knowledge of the more complex macramé was spread by travelers. No doubt some of the credit for spreading the technique to other parts of the world must be attributed to the missionaries of the religious orders. This credit must be shared with sailors, who found the craft a worthwhile way to spend idle hours of a long sea voyage. They usually worked with heavy materials such as cord or rope, and they made many useful and decorative trimmings such as mast skirts, picture frames, bunk pockets, and bell ropes. Captain Jack Shickell, Master Mariner (ret.), and former whaleman, now of the *Balclutha* of San Francisco, said:

"My own work was chiefly knotted fringes, both on bunk pockets (Fig. 1-8) and on sea-chest covers. Also on two

This bunk pocket knotted of white seine twine takes the place of a bedside table for a sailor. It is a handy place to keep a pipe, books, and other personal articles.(Courtesy of the Costume and Textile Study Collections, School of Home Economics, University of Washington)

FIGURE 1-8

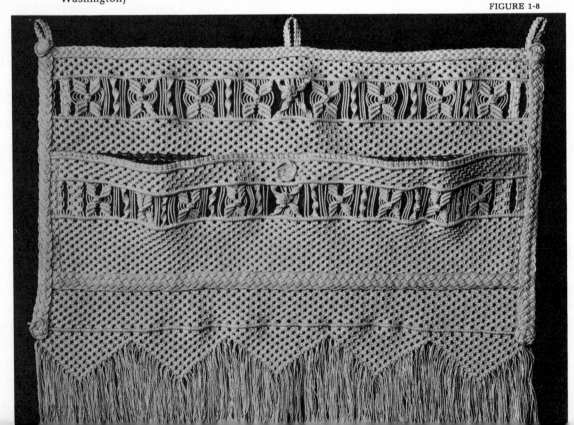

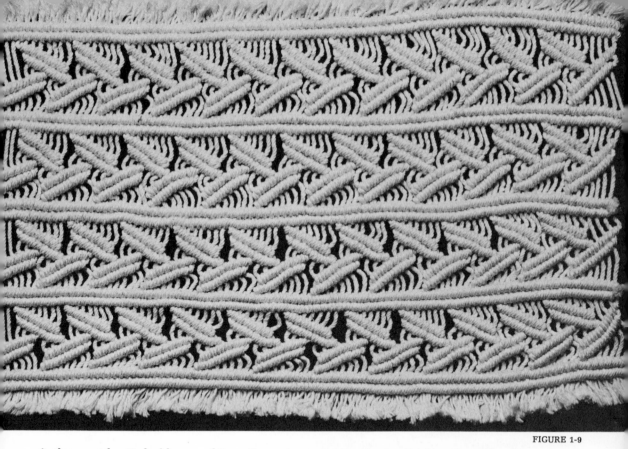

FIGURE 1-9

A place mat knotted of heavy white cotton seine twine by Charles Frisbie. (Courtesy of Betsy Frisbie Ekvall)

FIGURE 1-10

'Steward's baskets,' in which he carried the chow aft . . . or forward, from the galley. These baskets had to be covered to keep out the spray, and sometimes water more solid."

When Captain Shickell was asked for photographs of his work, he answered:

"I am sorry that I have nothing to offer by way of photographs . . . blame my own carelessness, or rather lack of interest in a thing after I have made it . . . the making of it being my joy. And, strange to say, I have very little of my own to show for it! It was traditional that sailing-ship men spent hours working on some gadget, and then gave it away to the first charmer ashore who admired it!"

In giving his knotting away, Captain Shickell was spreading a knowledge of the craft, just as other sailors had carried it to distant lands centuries before him. Knotted articles were used for barter by sailors

A small leaf pattern knotted in white wool makes a richly textured surface for this pillow.

15

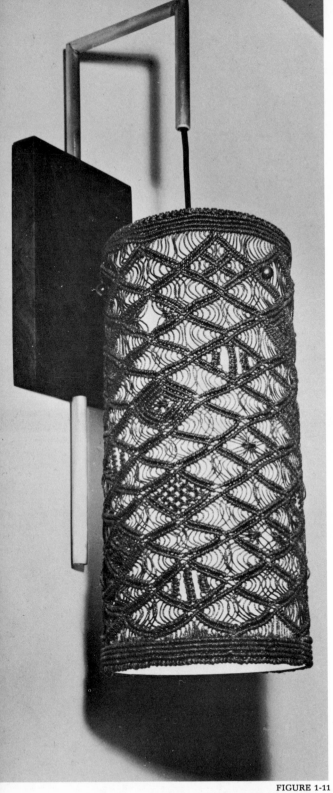

FIGURE 1-11

Light silhouettes the diamond pattern of macramé on this lamp shade. A waxed linen upholsterers' cord was used to make the cover for the plastic cylinder. 5½ inches in diameter, 12 inches long. (Wood and metal base by Donald W. Wheat)

when they went ashore on the China coast, in India, and in America.

Sailors frequently refer to their work as "Square Knotting" rather than macramé, and the Square Knot seems to be more predominant in their work than in the work of other knotters. They often use many other knots that are not included in the work that, strictly speaking, is called macramé. Sometimes they call it "Fancy rope work" (Figs. 1-30 and 1-31). Some references list the knotting as "McNamara's Lace," which tempts the imagination to speculate about a member of the sea-going fraternity named McNamara!

After a period of popularity in the late nineteenth and early twentieth centuries, macramé again faded into obscurity. This is understandable if you try to imagine a macramé fringe such as the one in Fig. 1-5 or 1-6 in the "moderne" room that was fashionable in the 1920's and 1930's. The styles were far too austere to accept anything so patterned as macramé. Now that fashions are removing some of the severity, it is possible to adapt the technique to objects that will enhance our homes and our garments, and form attractive accessories.

In the home macramé can be used for small articles such as place mats, pillow tops, lamp shades, upholstery (Figs. 1-9 through 1-16), or braids and trimmings (see Figs. 6-25 through 6-37). It forms an attractive pattern when it is hung in a see-through position, for example, as a room divider (Fig. 1-17) or window screen, or along an open stair well. Wall hangings offer an opportunity for endless variety because there are few design limitations dictated by their function. As long as they will stay on the wall and improve the space where they are hung, they fulfill their purpose (Figs. 1-18, 1-19, 1-20, and see Figs. 7-1, 7-18, 7-43, and 8-44). Free-hanging sculptural pieces are an exciting application of knotting (Figs. 1-21, 1-22, and see Figs. 7-45, 7-46, and 7-47). Mats or rugs are another possibility (see Fig. 8-54), although a large rug might be difficult to manage unless it were knotted in sections.

Macramé has its place in the garden too.

A knotted hanging on a garden wall or fence will enhance any patio (Fig. 1-23). For a more ambitious project, a hammock or replacements for the canvas on deck chairs might be knotted (Fig. 1-12).

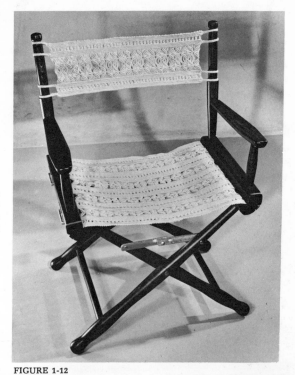

The back and seat of this director's chair were knotted with a tan linen upholsterers' twine. The solid areas of knotting cover cords that are attached to both sides of the chair to make the seat and back sturdy enough to support a person.

Detail from the back of the director's chair.

FIGURE 1-12

FIGURE 1-13

FIGURE 1-14

Detail from the seat of the director's chair.

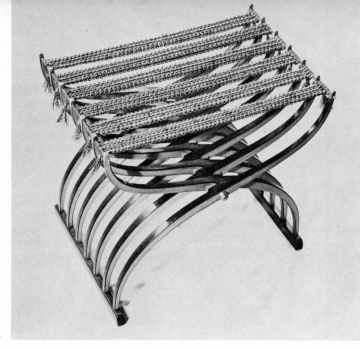

FIGURE 1-15

The seat of this small bench was knotted with brown nylon seine twine. The graceful X of the bench is repeated in the pattern of the knotting. (Bench designed and made by Evert Sodergren)

Detail from the knotting on the bench.

FIGURE 1-16

FIGURE 1-17

This knotted screen is part of the marine exhibit at the Museum of History and Industry in Seattle, Washington. It was knotted by Charles Frisbie. (Courtesy of the Museum of History and Industry and Betsy Frisbie Ekvall)

FIGURE 1-18

Small cork beads interspersed among the knots in this green cotton wall hanging make interesting accents in the composition. (Courtesy of Darlene Mapes)

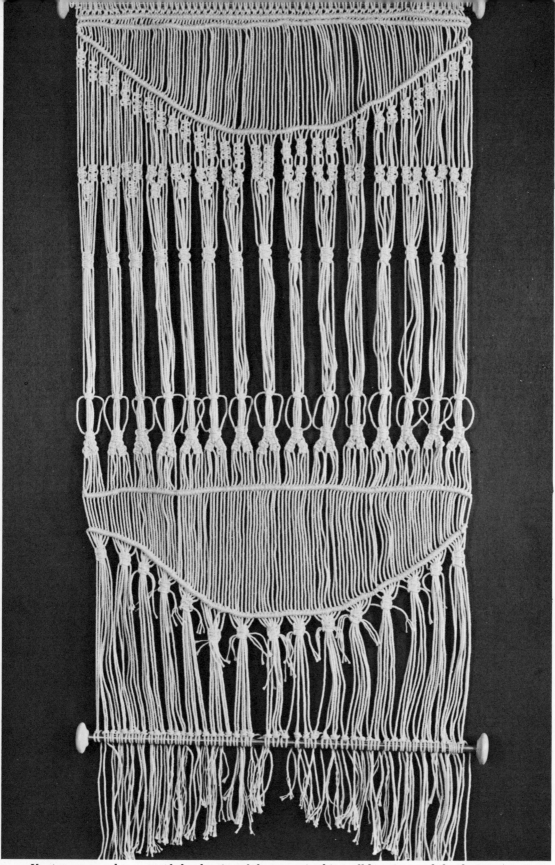

Knots were used to control the density of the yarns in this wall hanging, and the designer has used some of the ends as a part of her design. (Courtesy of Violet Olson)

FIGURE 1-19

21

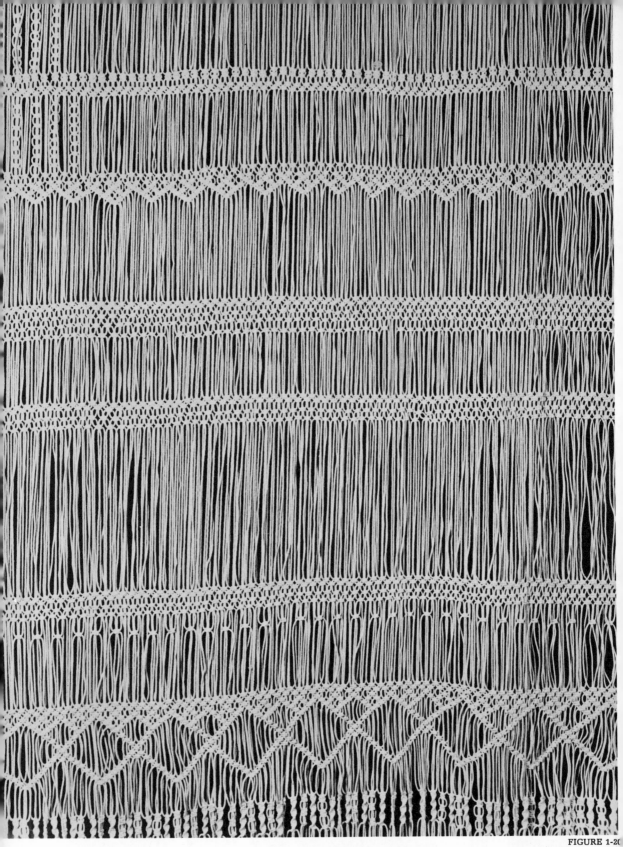

FIGURE 1-20

Knotting on a grand scale, this hanging was knotted from braided cotton cord by Spencer Dépas. 6 by 10 feet. (Photograph by Monika Reichelt)

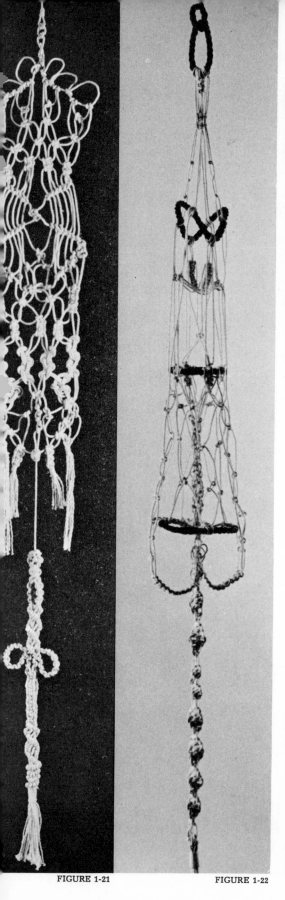

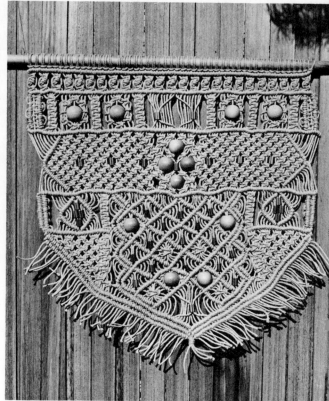

Top right. A garden hanging of heavy linen uphol-sterers' tufting twine. Small copper pieces found in a marine supply store and walnut-stained hard-wood beads were incorporated into the knotting. 23 by 24 inches.

Left. This free-hanging piece is a sculpture of cords and knots. (Knotted by LeRoy Schwarcz. Photo-graph by Albert C. Finn)

Center. Circles are used to give this free-hanging piece three-dimensional form. (Knotted by LeRoy Schwarcz. Photograph by June Schwarcz)

FIGURE 1-24

A sturdy tote bag knotted of yellow chalk line. (Courtesy of Stella W. Chen)

FIGURE 1-25

This silk evening bag was knotted with dark gold chainette purchased at a weavers' supply house. A mirror behind the bag shows the back of the bag. 4½ by 8 by 1¼ inches.

This eyeglass case was made with white nylon upholsterers' cord and lined with a padded fabric to protect the glasses. (Knotted by Gilda Van Norman)

FIGURE 1-26

Knotted articles are usually very sturdy, so macramé has long been a favorite technique for making accessories that receive hard wear, such as bags and belts, and small articles such as cases for cigarettes, cameras, or eyeglasses. The variety of styles and materials in which bags can be made is great. Students' book bags or sturdy bags for carrying parcels (Fig. 1-24) are very serviceable and attractive when knotted with heavy linen or sisal cord; fine silk or nylon will make a handsome evening purse (Fig. 1-25) or eyeglass case (Fig. 1-26). A bag you make for yourself is a joy because it can be planned to fit the things you carry, neither larger nor smaller than you need. Belts also offer a challenge to

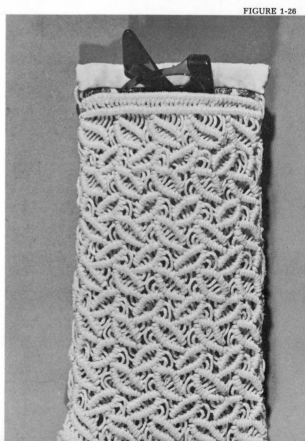

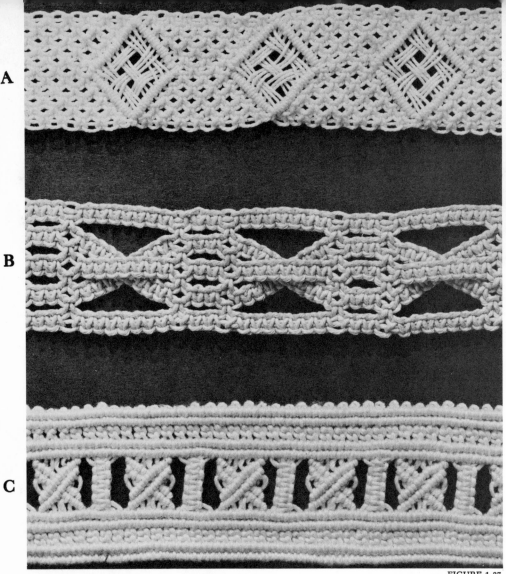

A

B

C

FIGURE 1-27

Belts *A* and *B* were made by knotting from the point of the belt toward the buckle. Belt *C* was knotted from the top edge toward the lower edge. The belts were knotted, respectively, of white nylon upholsterers' cord, yellow-tan linen upholsterers' cord, and soft cotton string similar to the string used by butchers.

the imagination. Emphasis can be placed either on color, as in the Mexican belts shown in Fig. C-2, or on pattern, as in the belts pictured in Fig. 1-27.

Articles of clothing are yet another possibility for the ambitious knotter. Since macramé can be knotted to shape (as explained in Chapter Eight), a garment can be made by knotting each piece over a pattern and then assembling the pieces. However, careful planning should precede any project of this size. In almost any yarn a closely knotted design will form a stiff

Right. A few knots and gay colored wool yarns are combined to make two belts from Mexico. The more solidly knotted belt was purchased in Colombia, South America, in 1948 by John H. Rowe, University of California, Berkeley.

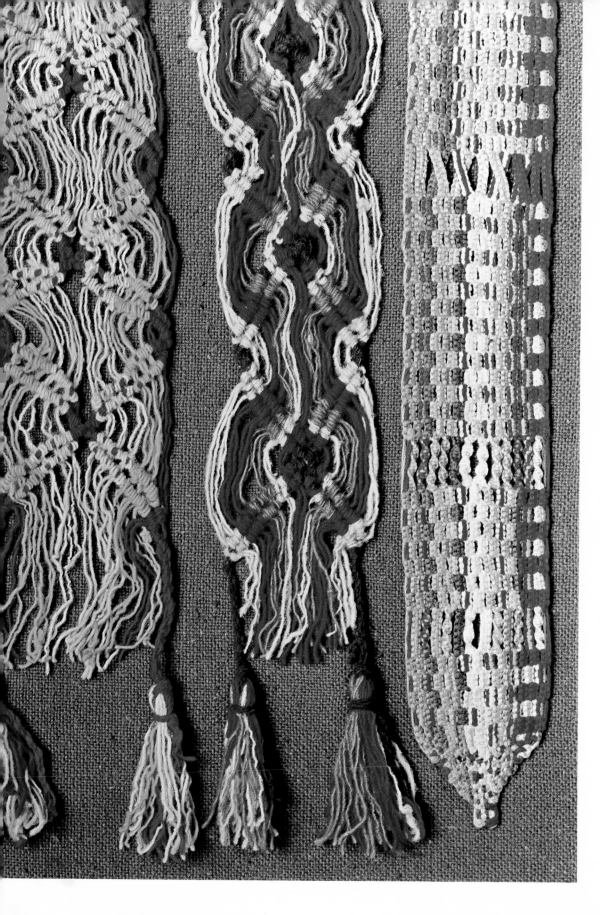

FIGURE 1-28

Macramé pull for a brass ship's bell, knotted from cotton seine twine by Charles Frisbie.
(Courtesy of Betsy Frisbie Ekvall and Bob Bollong)

FIGURE 1-29

A mast skirt near the overhead in the cabin, knotted of heavy white cotton twine by Charles Frisbie. (Courtesy of Betsy Frisbie Ekvall and Bob Bollong)

fabric. If a soft material is required, a pattern with spaced knots and a soft yarn should be selected. And since the knotting has an exciting texture, a simply styled garment that emphasizes the rich surface is a safe selection. A simple style is also easier to knot. If you wish a less ambitious undertaking, you might make a trimming or insertion for an already completed garment.

The enrichment of ecclesiastical garments and linens is as suitable today as it has been in centuries past. Macramé can be applied to the end of a stole, to the cuffs or edge of an alb, or to a cincture cord (Fig. 1-7). The evening skirt in Fig. C-3 has been enriched with knotted braids and small

pieces of macramé attached to the velvet with decorative stitchery.

Yachtsmen have many opportunities to use knotting, and frequently it serves a useful purpose as well as adding an air of tradition to their boats. A piece of rope would suffice for a bell pull (the handle that swings the clapper) but a macramé pull is more decorative (Fig. 1-28). A mast skirt (Fig. 1-29) absorbs any moisture that might leak into the cabin through a faulty seam. When a sailor finds that the mast skirt is wet, he knows he must recaulk around the mast or eventually it will rot. Macramé covering on the tiller handle gives the hand a better grip. Railing covers, such as the

FIGURE 1-30

Fancy rope work on the pulpit, knotted of cotton seine twine by Bob Bollong.

fancy rope work on the pulpit of the *Serene* (Figs. 1-30 and 1-31) reduce the amount of brass that must be polished. Deck chairs with knotted upholstery are also appropriate and practical. A boat with macramé is a cherished possession, because only a proud master would spend the time to make her more beautiful.

On land, knotting is well suited to the interiors of yacht clubs and other gathering-places for sailors or landlubbers who prefer a nautical décor. The Seattle Yacht Club has used it effectively, as may be seen in Figs. 1-32 and 1-33.

Many people have been introduced to knotting during an illness. Occupational therapists use it as a recreation and an exercise (sometimes they refer to it as "Cord Knotting"). Young people have learned it in groups such as the Boy Scouts, Girl Scouts, or Campfire Girls, and it is often part of the recreation program in childrens' camps. Since it requires very little equipment or storage space, it is an excellent craft to use when space and cost are major considerations.

It is impossible to enumerate all of the useful, decorative — and sometimes bizarre — pieces that can be made of macramé. I have heard of such diverse items as a golf bag, a bedspread, a baby-carriage cover, and a harness and trapping for a horse. Macramé is a technique that has limitations; however, with a careful choice of design and materials, it can be very versatile, practical, and beautiful.

FIGURE 1-31

Detail from Fig. 1-30.

FIGURE 1-33

The overhead light fixture in the entry hall of the Seattle Yacht Club filters the light through macramé. The knotting is silhouetted and makes a pleasant pattern of light and shadow. (Courtesy of the Seattle Yacht Club)

This room-divider at the Seattle Yacht Club was knotted of white cotton seine twine by Charles Frisbie. (Courtesy of Betsy Frisbie Ekvall and the Seattle Yacht Club)

FIGURE 1-32

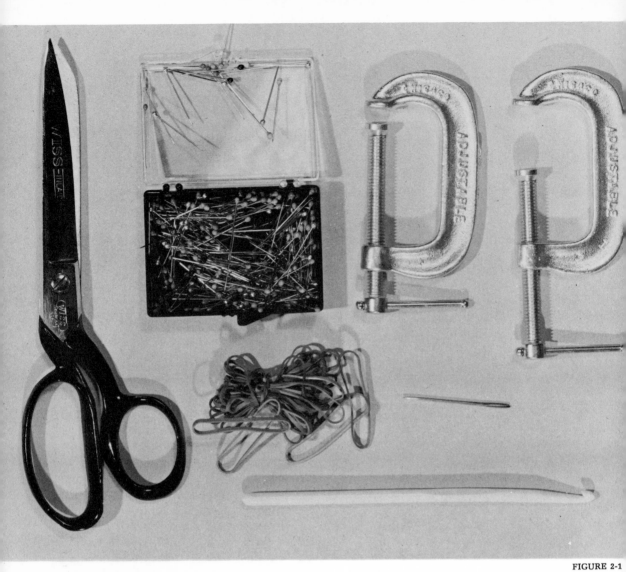

FIGURE 2-1

Tools for macramé: scissors, pins, C-clamps, rubber bands, yarn needle, crochet hook.

2

TOOLS

The basic tools needed for macramé are shown in Fig. 2-1. Scissors, pins, and a working surface are the only tools you need for many knotting projects. Occasionally a crochet hook or a yarn needle is useful, and rubber bands or small bobbins are used to keep long knotting cords in bundles that are easier to handle (see Figs. 4-11 and 4-12). Sometimes a C-clamp is used to hold some of the cords taut as you knot. For instance, it is helpful when you are tying many Square Knots or making braids. If a C-clamp is attached to the bottom edge of the knotting board, the shank will provide a place to fasten your cords (Fig. 2-2). Sailors frequently use a hook that is tied around the waist.

Knotters have used a variety of working surfaces; one example is a weighted pillow like that in Fig. 2-3. A padded brick makes a similar working surface. One woman, from Mitla, Mexico, used no base at all: her technique is pictured in Fig. 2-4. It is difficult to say that one device is better than another. In many cases the base you use will depend upon the article to be knotted and your own working comfort and surroundings. Any weighted base, such as the pillow, or a stationary base that attaches to a wall or a table is desirable because it will hold the work steady when the cords are pulled to tighten the knots. However, you may prefer to sacrifice weight for portability (I like to carry my work with me and knot during those odd moments when it is necessary to wait for someone or something). Any rigid surface that you can pin into, such as a clipboard with a pad attached (Fig. 2-2), a piece of polyurethane foam (Fig. 2-5), beaverboard, or padded cardboard (Figs. 2-6 and 2-7), makes a lightweight and portable base.

Occupational therapists have developed a variety of working bases with devices to hold some of the cords taut (Figs. 2-8, 2-9, and 2-10).

If your project is a long one or the yarns are heavy, the completed part of your knotting may be heavy enough to hold the work in place without a base. For other projects with heavy yarns, it is necessary to have a sturdy support. When the garden hanging of heavy linen shown in Fig. 1-23 was knotted, an easel supported the work.

In any project the working surface must be adapted to the shape of the finished article. When knotting continuously around a piece, for example, it must be possible to work on all sides. The white jute bag in Figs. 2-11 and 2-12 was attached to its leather bottom at the beginning and then supported on a block of wood that had the same dimensions as the finished bag. The lamp shade in Fig. 1-11 is another piece that was knotted continuously. The inner plastic cylinder that forms a permanent part of the shade also served as a working base. Knotting over a base that is the same size as the completed piece also helps to keep the work from drawing in as it progresses.

FIGURE 2-2

A folded towel attached to a clipboard serves as a base for knotting. A C-clamp holds the center cords taut.

FIGURE 2-3

FIGURE 2-4

A sand-stuffed pillow serves as a weighted base that remains stationary when the cords are pulled taut during the knotting. (From *Tools and Toys of Stitchery* by Gertrude Whiting, Cambridge University Press, 1928)

A woman from Mitla, Mexico, knotting a *rebozo*, or shawl. The weight of the finished knotting that is rolled and placed on the table holds the work in place as she knots. (From "Macramé in Mitla" by Marjorie Cordley Rouillion. Courtesy of *Craft Horizons*, November/December 1953)

A polyurethane foam pad, sold as a kneeling pad in variety stores, forms a portable working surface.

FIGURE 2-5

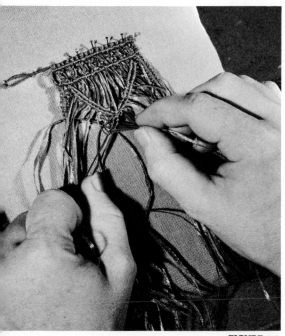

FIGURE 2-6

A piece of cardboard padded with layers of outing flannel and covered with a scrap of linen provides a very small working surface to tuck under your arm or in your purse so you can snatch a moment for knotting occasionally.

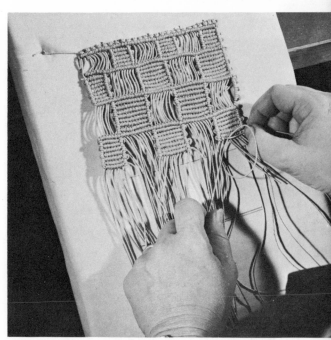

FIGURE 2-7

A piece of stiff cardboard padded with polyurethane foam and covered with cotton sheeting is used as a base. The lines marked on the surface of the covering are a guide to keep the work square and straight.

FIGURE 2-8

A portable wood frame used by occupational therapists. A clamp, A, holds the knotting; another device, B, holds the two center cords taut as the knot is tied over them. (Courtesy of Ruth M. Peterson, O.R.T.)

FIGURE 2-10

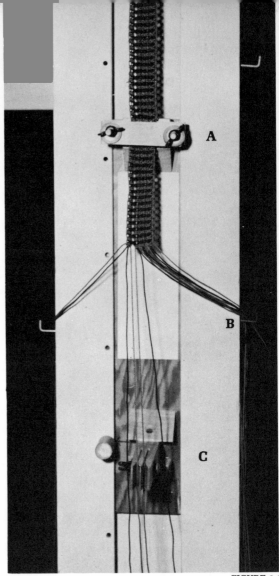

FIGURE 2-9

This frame used by occupational therapists is attached to the wall so the knotter can stand or sit on a stool when he works. A marks the clamp that holds the knotting, B indicates the hooks that hold the unused cords out of the way, and the notched device at C holds the two center cords taut. (Courtesy of the State of Washington, Department of Labor and Industries, Dr. H. T. Buckner, Rehabilitation Center for Injured Workers)

An upright frame used by occupational therapists holds large objects as they are knotted. The knotter stands or sits on a stool as he works. A C-clamp, A, holds unused cords out of the way. One clamp is placed on each side of the work and moved down as the knotting progresses. A board, B, has a series of notches cut in it. The center cords are placed in these notches so they will be held taut. (Courtesy of the State of Washington Department of Labor and Industries, Dr. H. T. Buckner Rehabilitation Center for Injured Workers)

FIGURE 2-11

A knotter begins a bag with a leather bottom. She holds the work in position by placing it over a block of wood and works from the base toward the top. (Courtesy of Carol Otness)

FIGURE 2-12

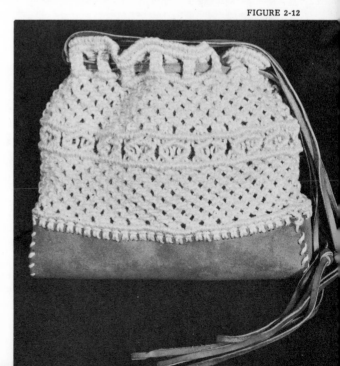

The finished bag. White jute was used for the knotting. (Courtesy of Carol Otness)

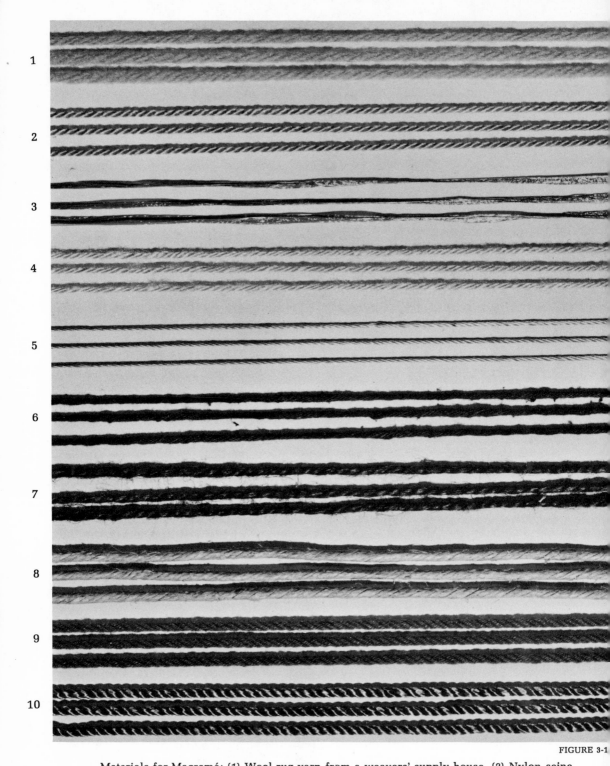

FIGURE 3-1

Materials for Macramé: (1) Wool rug yarn from a weavers' supply house. (2) Nylon seine twine, size 18, from a marine supply store. (3) Viscose straw from a weavers' supply house. (4) *Avisco* rayon "All Purpose Yarn" from a variety store. (5) Nylon floss from a marine supply store. (6) Cotton wrapping twine used by a department store. (7) Jute yarn from a weavers' supply house. (8) Linen spring twine from an upholsterers' supply house. (9) Cabled cotton seine twine, 4-ply, 7 strands, from a marine supply store. (10) Cabled nylon seine twine, size 48, continuous filament, from a marine supply store.

3

MATERIALS FOR MACRAME

A search in the cupboards of most households will uncover some materials that can be used for knotting. Attractive articles can be made from many of the multitude of cords, twines, strings, lines, and yarns that are manufactured (Figs. 3-1 through 3-9). These materials are found in hardware stores, grocery stores, marine suppliers, hobby shops, knitting shops, weavers' suppliers, surplus stores, and some drug stores — and in many unexpected places. After you have started knotting, you will begin to inspect any string or cord you encounter more closely, and you may be surprised to find an interesting material lying on the shelf of a store, tying up a package, or strung as support for someone's sweet peas! If the cord you find is in use, your search for a place to buy it may resemble a detective story.

It took me several months to discover where to purchase a handsome yellow-tan waxed linen cord that had been tied around some moving parts of a loom to hold them stationary during shipment to me. I carried the cord in my pocket and asked questions of everyone I met who might know what it was. Finally someone told me that it looked like upholsterers' tufting twine, and I found that it could be purchased at an upholsterers' supply store. It was worth the search — it is an excellent knotting material that was used for many of the illustrations in this book.

Traditionally, macramé has been knotted from hard-twisted cotton, linen, or silk cord. However, any yarn can be used that will survive the abrasive action of the knotting and the tension that occurs when the knots are tightened. Some materials cause more problems than others. Slippery or very springy yarns may not hold a knot, and some poor-grade yarns are not worth the investment of your time. Knotters usually avoid yarns with great elasticity, and there is no doubt that a hard-twisted cord with no loops, thick and thin places, or other irregular surfaces will best show the pattern of the knotting. Since the outstanding characteristic of macramé is the textural quality of the knots as they are arranged to form pattern, it is difficult to introduce too many more elements into a piece successfully. Many colors or elaborate yarns or both usually result in confusion rather than in a well-ordered, attractive design. This is not to say that a very skillful designer could not combine all three elements successfully, but generally it is best to choose a yarn that is simple in color and composition, and let the textural quality of the technique dominate.

The material you choose should be selected carefully to fit the project you are planning. A strong linen cord with a hard twist will make a bag that holds its shape well and withstands hard wear. The size of the yarn is important in choosing material

FIGURE 3-2

Avisco rayon "All Purpose Yarn" (#4, page 38).

FIGURE 3-3

Viscose straw (#3, page 38).

Wool rug yarn (#1, page 38).

FIGURE 3-4

for a screen or room-divider because you are more concerned with the silhouette of the yarn than with its ability to wear. The quality of stiffness and firmness that makes a hard-twisted linen cord desirable for a bag or belt makes it undesirable for most wearing apparel. For a garment you would probably choose a wool that does not have very much elasticity, or a silk yarn. The pattern of knotting also has an influence on the suppleness of the garment. It is easier to make a hard, firm fabric with

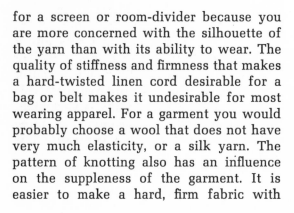

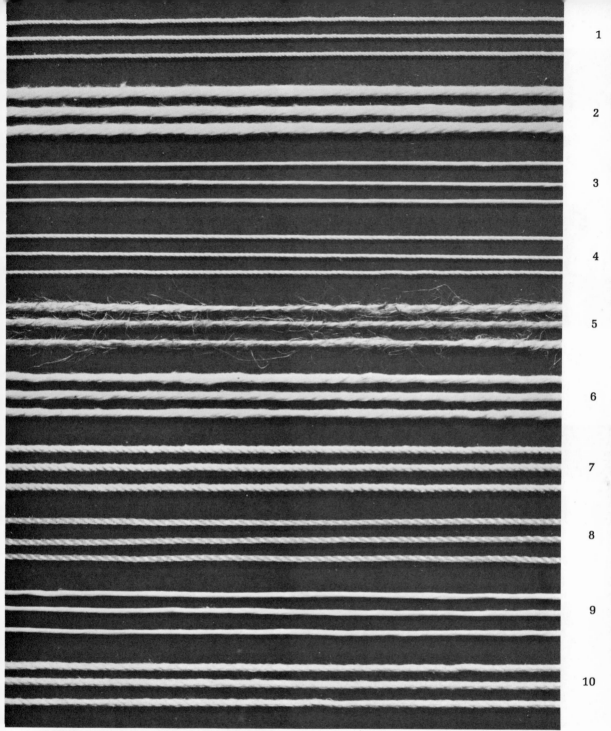

FIGURE 3-5

(1) Cotton seine twine from a marine supply house.
(2) Cotton "Rug Weave Yarn" from a weavers' supply house.
(3) Linen tufting twine from an upholsterers' supply house.
(4) Cotton "Belfast Cord," also known as "Dreadnaught Cord," from a weavers' supply house.
(5) Jute wrapping twine from a hardware store.
(6) Cotton butcher twine from a butcher shop.
(7) Cotton chalk line from a hardware store.
(8) Polyethylene cord from a weavers' supply house.
(9) Linen cord, size 12, from a weavers' supply house.
(10) Linen cord, size 12/18, from a weavers' supply house.

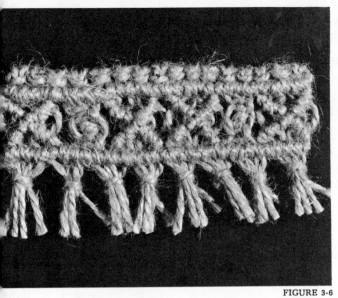

FIGURE 3-6

Jute wrapping twine (#5,page 41).

FIGURE 3-7

Linen cord, size 12 (#9 ,page 41).

FIGURE 3-9

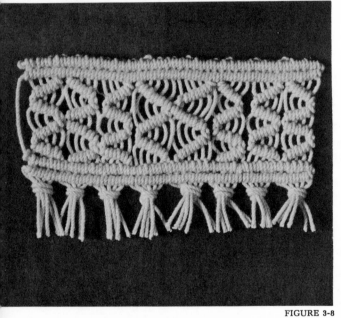

FIGURE 3-8

Cotton seine twine (#1,page 41).

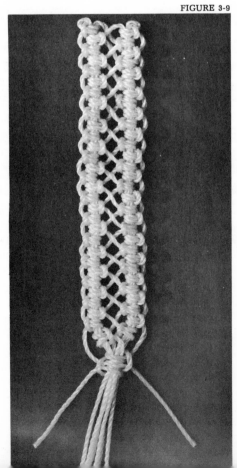

Polyethylene cord (#8 ,page 41).

FIGURE 3-10   FIGURE 3-11

Two pieces knotted in the same patterns with different materials. One (*left*) is a nylon seine twine; the other (*right*) is a soft-twist cotton butcher twine. The upper pattern consists of Square Knots in alternate arrangement; the lower pattern is made with a Square Knot plus a Half Knot in alternate arrangement (see Fig. 7-5).

knotting than to find a combination of yarn and pattern that will combine well for a soft, supple fabric. The pillow-top material in Fig. 1-10 would make a handsome sweater-jacket, and the Mexican stole knotted in wool in Fig. 2-4 drapes very well, partly because of the yarn and partly because an open pattern was chosen for the knotting.

The combined qualities of twist, size, and fiber are important in choosing a knotting material. Figs 3-10 and 3-11 show the dif-

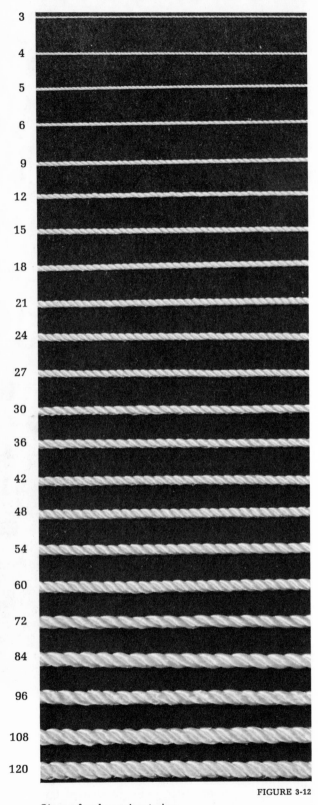

3
4
5
6
9
12
15
18
21
24
27
30
36
42
48
54
60
72
84
96
108
120

Sizes of nylon seine twine.

FIGURE 3-12

ference that twist makes in the appearance of knotting. The size of yarn you choose depends upon the scale of the piece you are planning to knot. Yarns come in many sizes, as you can see in Fig. 3-12, which shows the sizes of nylon seine twine. Many knotters seem to favor cords about the size of numbers 15 and 18. Most of the illustrations in Chapter Seven were made with cords approximately this size. However, for a large-scale piece, such as a hanging, a room-divider, or a rug, you might choose a larger cord.

There are yarns in almost all fibers, natural or man-made, that are useful to the knotter, and conversely, there are some yarns in each group that are not wise choices. In general, linen is one of the most desirable materials. The color range is limited in the size and twist most useful to knotters, but the yarns that are available have a soft sheen and a handsome appearance. They produce an attractive, long wearing, dirt resistant piece, and the extra expense of the material is justified when you consider the time involved in the knotting.

Jute and sisal are comparable to linen in many ways, and these yarns are usually less expensive than most other materials. They have good wearing quality, and there is a wide selection of color and size. Most of these yarns do not have the smooth texture of linen and the knotted patterns will therefore not be as crisp and clear-cut as a pattern knotted in linen. However, sometimes a less sophisticated appearance is desirable.

The selection of cotton yarns, lines, strings, twines, and cords is almost endless. They come in dull or shiny, large or small, hard or soft twists — and even in braided form, like Venetian-blind cord. The color selection is the best of any of the yarns. However, cotton does not resist soil as well as some of the other materials, so it is advisable to use it for articles that are washable.

Some wool yarns will knot very well, but care must be taken in their selection. There are so many different kinds that it is impossible to be specific about them here. If you plan to use a wool yarn for a project, the only way to be sure of your material is to make a sample in the knotting pattern you plan to use. The yarn should complement the pattern, and the pattern should allow the yarn to show its good qualities. You may find that a very elastic yarn is difficult to knot, and it is tricky to keep the correct tension so the completed article is the desired shape. (Wool rug yarns usually have less elasticity than knitting yarns.) Many beautiful things can be made from wool, so don't be timid about using it — just plan your article carefully before you start and be sure you have selected the best yarn for the purpose.

There are so many man-made yarns that, as with wool, it is not possible to be specific about them here. Some of them are made from a mixture of man-made materials alone; others combine natural and man-made fibers. The time is past when yarns like nylon and rayon were synonymous with slippery, shiny materials. Now some of the man-made yarns simulate the natural fibers in both appearance and other qualities, and each must be judged on its own merits. Just as we judge people, so should we judge a yarn — not for the name it carries, but for the qualities and the characteristics of the yarn itself. If you take the time to get acquainted with a yarn, you may find hidden qualities.

Even a slippery-looking yarn should not be ruled out without a trial. I have heard knotters say: "Nylon can't be used for knotting — it slips." This is true for some nylon yarns as well as some of the other man-made yarns, but not for all of them. In fact, there is an attractive white nylon upholsterers' tufting twine that lists the claim "no-slip knot" on the box. Most of the fishermen's netting cords are nylon, and some of them knot very well. An experienced knotter may be able to use a yarn even though it slips. The bag shown in Fig. 3-13 was made with nylon that did not hold a knot very well and unraveled when it was cut. To stop the unraveling, the end of each cord was melted slightly by holding

it briefly over a flame. As the work progressed, the knotter tightened the knots in the previous row, so each knot was held in place by the row that followed. The bag was tedious to make, but the result was worth the extra effort.

The polyethylene cord shown in Figs. 3-5 (8) and 3-9 has a glossy surface and a stiff quality that might cause it to be rejected as a knotting material without a trial. But the very stiffness that makes it questionable actually gives the knotted piece more firmness and causes it to hold a shape better than most cords. When it is knotted, the cord has a translucent quality and a waxy feel that is very pleasant.

FIGURE 3-13

Dark blue nylon cord was used for this bag. The front and back were started over the rods for the brass handles. A separate piece was knotted for the bottom and sides, and the bag was assembled when the knotting was completed. (Courtesy of Marrietta M. Ward)

45

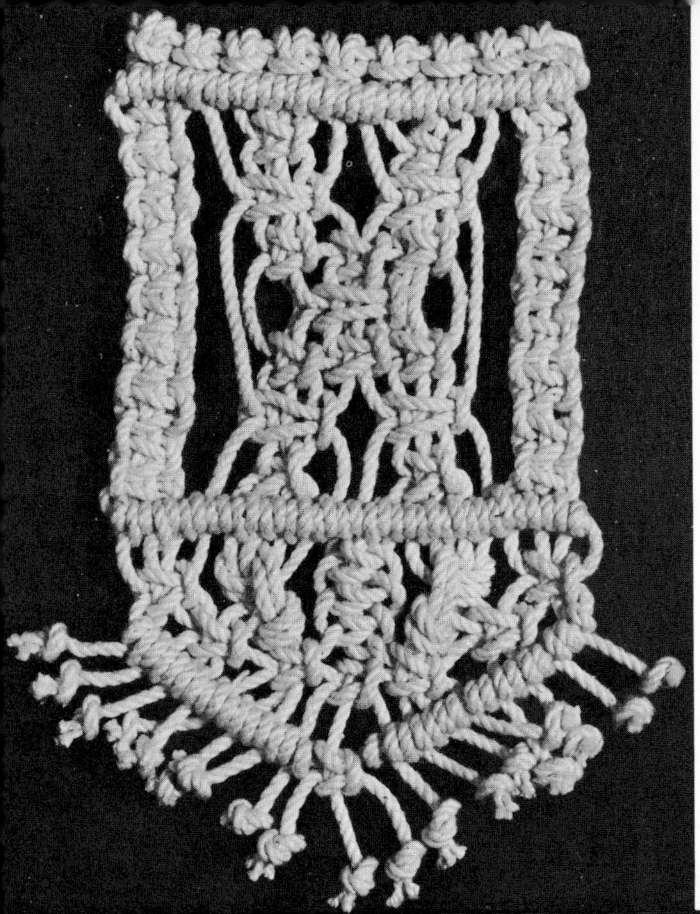

FIGURE 3-14

A sample made of yellow chalk line.

A sample of cabled linen, size 12/18.

FIGURE 3-15

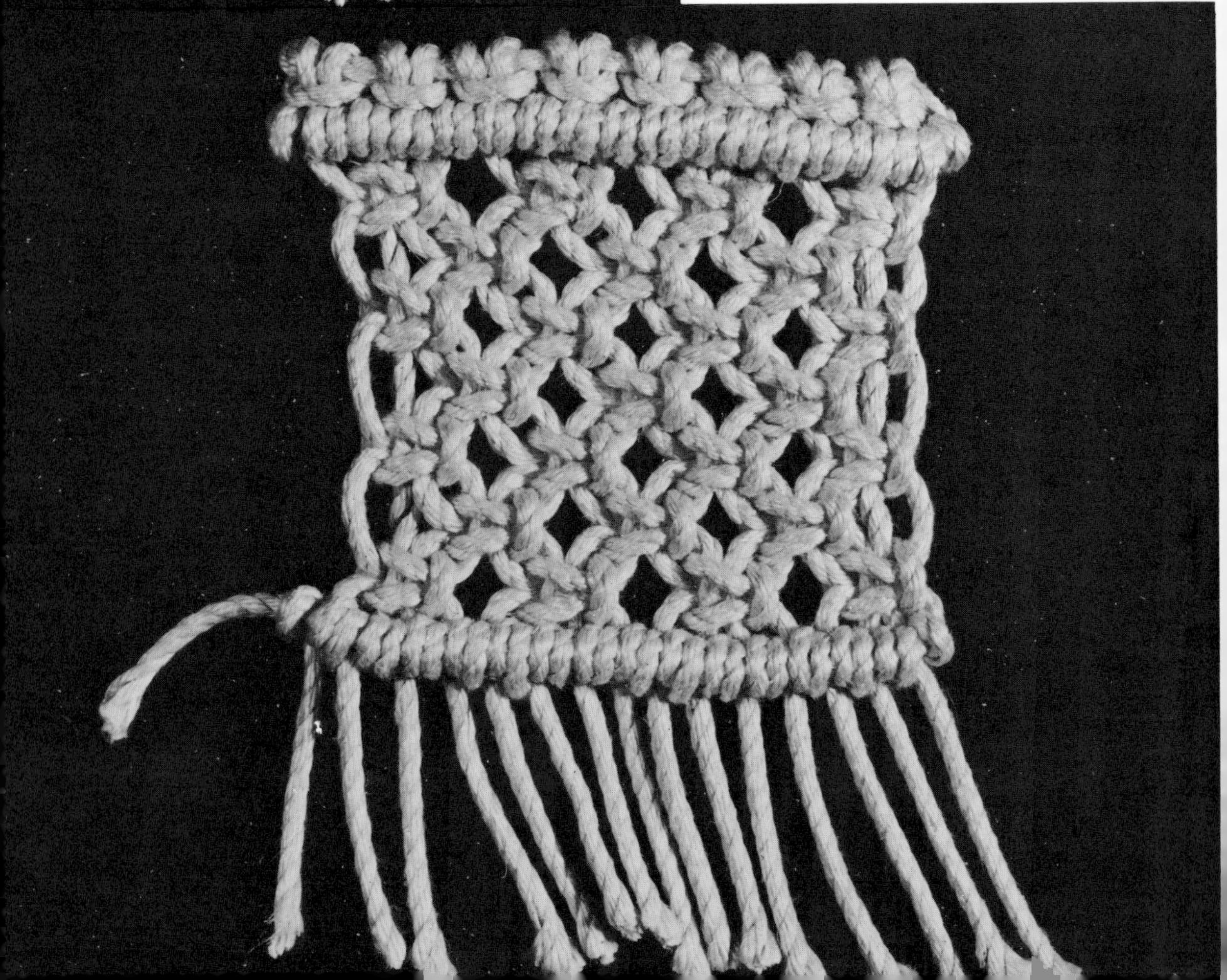

It is worth investing a little time to make a sample of a new cord. A piece three or four inches square should show you how the material handles, how it looks, and what kind of knotted designs are most suited to it, and will also serve as a gauge for planning future projects (Figs. 3-2, 3-4, 3-14, and 3-15). Attach the sample to a card and note on the card the name of the material, the kind of fiber, the place you found it, and its cost. You will have a permanent record for future reference. If you also record the number of cords per inch in the sample, it will be a simple matter to calculate the amount of material and the number of cords you need to prepare for a project made in the sample yarn and pattern.

The information in this chapter on materials is very general for several reasons. Some people work well with a material that is not successful for others. It is far better that you explore the possibilities for yourself. Part of the fun of knotting is searching for the materials to use and then testing them to see if they will work.

The crispness of a plastic-coated tire cord gives the pattern of this bag an attractive precision. (Courtesy of Jacqueline Enthoven)

FIGURE 3-16

FIGURE 4-1

Two C-clamps attached to a table form a simple device for measuring strands to be cut for knotting.

4

PREPARATION FOR KNOTTING

After you have assembled your equipment and chosen your material, the next step is the preparation of the material. The length and number of cords are determined by the size of the article you intend to make. A sample, at least three inches square, should be knotted, using the materials and pattern you plan to use. Count the ends per inch in the sample and multiply this number by the width of the article you expect to knot to determine the number of cords you must measure and cut. In nearly every case all of the cords will be the same length.

One of the most puzzling questions in knotting is what length the cords should be cut. For the average project the cords should be three and a half or four times the length of the finished piece. Since, as will be seen, you usually start a project with cords that have been doubled, each cord should actually measure seven or eight times the length of the finished project. It is very difficult, and in some places impossible, to add a new cord if you run out before you have completed a piece. It is therefore advisable to measure the cords carefully and generously. This is not the time to be a string saver! (However, we all miscalculate occasionally, so a few ways to replace a cord are explained on page 114.)

Some materials and some patterns require more length than others. Usually a thick cord takes up more length in knotting than a fine one, and the amount of take-up depends upon the size of the cord. Again, when you work with unusual materials, sampling with yarns that have been measured both before and after they are knotted is the only way to determine the length the cords should be cut.

Cords of equal length can be measured in many different ways. Two doorknobs that are the correct distance apart work very well to wind the cord around. C-clamps provide one of the most flexible methods of measuring (Fig. 4-1). They can be attached to many different surfaces and adjusted so the cords are measured the exact length desired.

After the cords are measured, they are mounted on the working surface with a *holding cord*. The holding cord does exactly what its name implies. It holds all of the cords in place so the work can be started, and it is fastened to the working surface at each end with a pin. It should be cut about six inches longer than the width of the piece you expect to knot, to allow three inches on each end for the knot the pin will pass through to fasten the holding cord down.

Each cord is mounted on the holding cord by folding it in half and attaching it with a Reversed Double Half Hitch, as shown in the following four steps:

1. The knotting cord is folded, bringing ends A and E together (Fig. 4-2).

2. The top of the loop C is brought down over the cords A and E, forming loops B and D (Fig. 4-3).

3. B and D are folded back until they are touching. This wraps C around the two cords A and E (Fig. 4-4).

4. The holding cord X-Y is placed through loops B and D, and the knot is tightened by pulling firmly on A and E (Fig. 4-5).

FIGURE 4-4

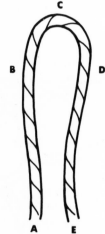

FIGURE 4-2

FIGURE 4-5

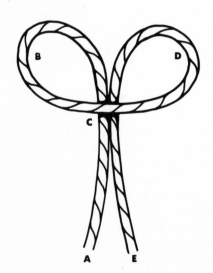

FIGURE 4-3

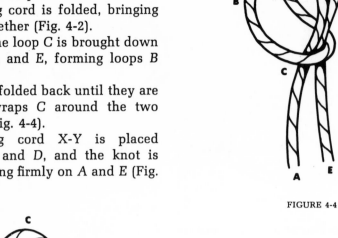

FIGURE 4-6

50

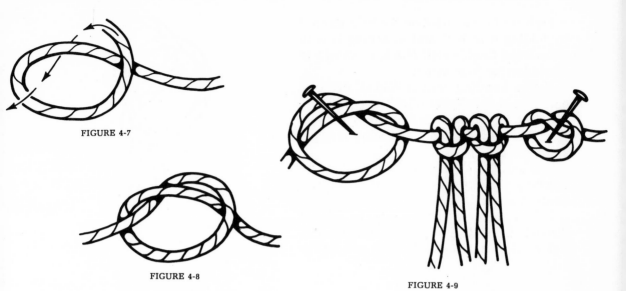

FIGURE 4-7

FIGURE 4-8

FIGURE 4-9

Each successive knotting cord is placed on the holding cord in the same way (Fig. 4-6). For most patterns they should fit snugly next to one another, neither crowded too closely nor spaced too far apart.

After all of the cords are mounted, an Overhand Knot is placed in each end of the mounting cord:

The Overhand Knot is tied by forming a loop near the end of the cord (Fig. 4-7); the end of the cord is then wrapped around the cord and pulled through the loop (Fig. 4-8).

The holding cord is attached to the working surface by pushing a pin through each knot and pinning it down securely. Fig. 4-9 shows the knot at the left end of the cord before it has been tightened over the pin, and the right-hand knot after it has been tied more firmly. These Overhand Knots should be placed near the group of knotting cords, and the holding cord should be taut and securely pinned so the work is well anchored.

This method of mounting and beginning is suitable for many projects. However, there are many other ways to start, and some of them are explained in Chapter Eight. You will want to use the mounting that suits your project best.

When the size of the piece you are planning to knot requires very long cords, it is necessary to reduce their length to knot with them. Some knotters use a looped chain to shorten a cord (Fig. 4-10):

FIGURE 4-10

Loop A is pulled through loop B and another loop is made in the cord and pulled through loop A, continuing thus until all of the cord is shortened. The chaining should start at the end of the cord and proceed toward the knotting. The looped chain is then fastened so it will not come loose or unchained until the knotting has progressed to the point where you need more cord.

A cord can be made into a small bobbin

51

Starting to wrap a bobbin that will be fastened with a rubber band.

FIGURE 4-11

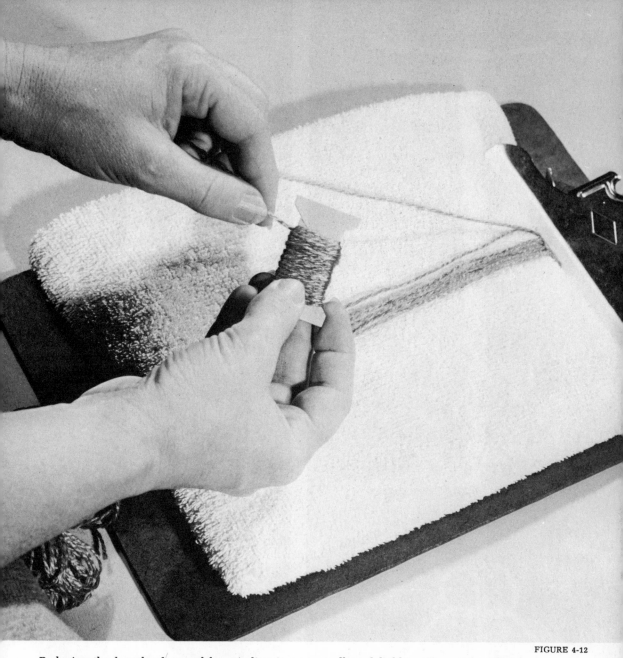

FIGURE 4-12

Reducing the length of a cord by winding it on a cardboard bobbin. The cord will be pulled into the small slit in the cardboard (just next to the end being wound) to keep it from unwinding during the knotting.

and fastened with a rubber band to make it easier to handle. If these bundles are wound by starting near the knotting and winding toward the end of the cord, the cord will feed out as you knot without removing the rubber band and rewinding the bundle (Fig. 4-11).

Small bobbins can be made of wood or cardboard to hold the cords. Plastic bob-bins that are used to hold yarn are available where knitting yarns are sold. These bobbins must be wrapped by starting at the end of the cord and wrapping toward the knotting so the cord will feed off the bobbin as the work progresses (Fig. 4-12). A slit can be cut in the edge of the bobbin to keep the cord from unwinding during the knotting.

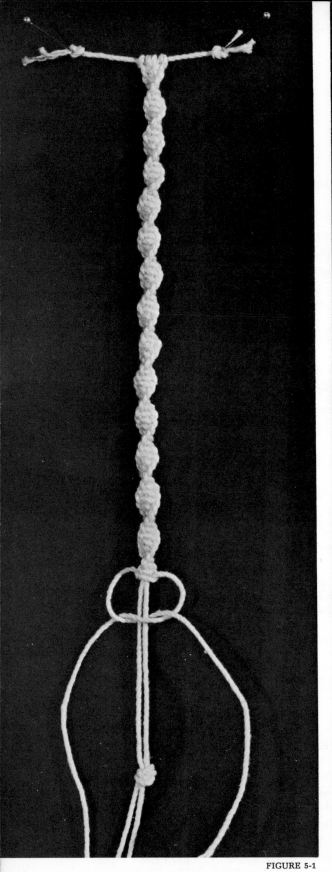

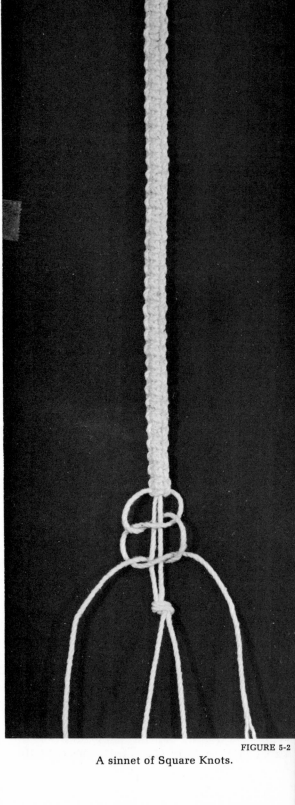

FIGURE 5-1

FIGURE 5-2

A sinnet of Half Knots.

A sinnet of Square Knots.

5

LEARNING THE BASIC KNOTS

It is difficult to believe, when you see an elaborate design in macramé, that most of it has been knotted with two simple knots, the Square Knot and the Double Half Hitch. The variation is achieved by the way they are tied and the way they are combined.

The Square Knot is tied in two parts (there is a method of tying both parts in one operation that is explained on page 58), and each part is called the Half Knot. When the Half Knot is tied repeatedly, a spirally twisted cord or *sinnet*, as it is called by sailors, is created (Fig. 5-1). When the Square Knot is tied repeatedly, a flat sinnet is formed (Fig. 5-2).

It is best to start on small practice pieces because the strands you use are short and easy to handle. Tying a few knots in a sample will give you the feel of the knotting. You will learn the easiest way for you to handle the knotting cords, and how much tension is needed to keep the work uniform when you tighten the knots.

Mason line is the material recommended for making the samples below. It is an inexpensive white string, about the same size as number 18 in Fig. 3-12, and it is frequently sold as a wrapping twine. It is slightly finer than the yellow chalk line that is sold in hardware stores. (Of course, any material can be used for your samples, but a hard-twisted, inexpensive twine like Mason line is better for learning the knots. If you use a larger size of twine, cut longer cords.)

Before you start, a word of caution should be given regarding the length of the cords that are required. The measurements

have been calculated very carefully so you will have enough cord to complete the samples *if you follow the directions carefully and if you knot firmly. Read the directions first, then follow the diagrams.* Now, let's try the Half Knot.

DIRECTIONS FOR A SINNET OF HALF KNOTS (FIG. 5-1)

Cut two strands of Mason line 48 inches long.
Cut one strand of Mason line 4 inches long for a holding cord.

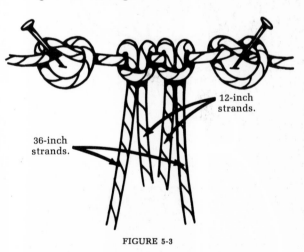

12-inch strands.

36-inch strands.

FIGURE 5-3

Fold the long strands so one end is 12 inches long and the other is 36 inches long, and loop them on the holding cord with Reversed Double Half Hitches (see page 50) so the two 12-inch strands are in the center and the two 36-inch strands are on the outside. Place an Overhand Knot (see page 51) at each end of the holding cord and pin it to your knotting board (Fig. 5-3).

The four cords are numbered from left to right. Cords 2 and 3 are *filler cords*, and, since they remain stationary when you knot this sample, they should be attached to a holder at the bottom of your knotting board (see Fig. 2-2). It is much easier to tie the knots over them if they are held taut. The two outside cords, 1 on the left and 4 on the right, are called *knotting cords*, and these are knotted over and under the filler cords.

To Tie the Half Knot:

Place the right-hand cord 4 over cords 2 and 3 and leave it in that position (Fig. 5-4).

Pick up the left-hand cord 1 and place it over cord 4, then bend it around 4 so it

goes under cords 2 and 3 and diagonally up through the space between cords 3 and 4.

Pull cords 1 and 4 firmly to tighten the knot (Fig. 5-5). This same knot is repeated (Fig. 5-6) until the knotting cords are used up or a 6-inch length of the work is finished. As the work spirals, it is occasionally necessary to transfer the knotting cords to opposite sides. The spiral will twist to the left when the first half of the Square Knot is tied; the second half of the Square Knot, explained below, will produce a right-hand twist.

FIGURE 5-6

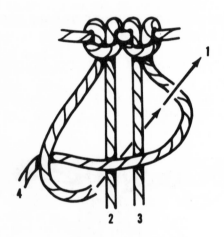

FIGURE 5-4

DIRECTIONS FOR A SINNET OF SQUARE KNOTS (FIG. 5-2)

The Square Knot is made in two operations. The first part of the knot is tied exactly as you tied the Half Knot in the first sample. To make a sample to learn and practice the Square Knot, first follow the directions for the sample sinnet of Half Knots. Prepare the strands for knotting in the same way and fasten them to your knotting board.

To Tie the Square Knot:

Tie the first part of the knot by following the directions for the Half Knot. Now we come to the second half of the knot.

Place the right-hand cord 1 under cords 2 and 3 horizontally and leave it in that position (Fig. 5-7).

FIGURE 5-5

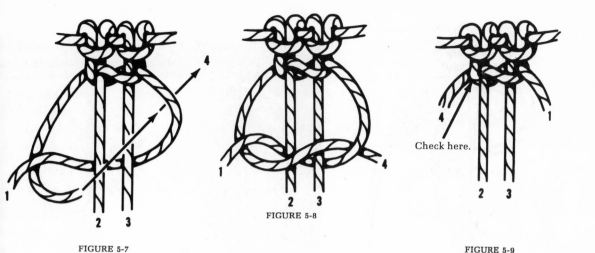

FIGURE 5-8

FIGURE 5-7

Check here.

FIGURE 5-9

Pick up the left-hand cord 4 and place it under the right-hand cord 1; then bend it around cord 1 and lay it over cords 2 and 3 diagonally, so it goes down through the loop between 3 and 1. Pull cords 1 and 4 firmly to tighten the knot (Fig. 5-8).

The Square Knot is always composed of the two knots you have just learned, tied alternately. Either part of the knot can be tied first and they will still form a Square Knot. Thus, when you knot the practice sinnet of Square Knots, the first and second parts of the knot are alternated. If your work is interrupted, you may forget which part of the knot comes next. The following rule will help you avoid an error and continue with the correct knot:

If the last cord on the left comes *under* the loop on the left, then the next cord on the right goes *under* the filler cords. If the last cord on the left comes *over* the loop on the left, then the next cord on the right goes *over* the filler cords.

In Fig. 5-9, where it is marked "Check here," the cord on the left — cord 4 — comes *under* the loop; therefore, the cord on the right — cord 1 — goes under the filler cords 2 and 3 to start the next part of the knot.

Your sample will look like the flat sinnet shown in Fig. 5-2. If, after making some samples, you want to knot a useful article, either of the knots could be used to make a dog leash or, perhaps, a tie-belt for a dress. If you look carefully at Fig. 4-11, you will notice that the knotter's wrist watch band is a flat sinnet.

It is possible to tie the two parts of the Square Knot in one operation. Figs. 5-10 through 5-14 show the five steps in tying this knot. In Fig. 5-10 loops A and B are passed under the two center cords and then over the cord at C. Step four is the trick in tying the knot. When you learn the correct cords to pull, the Square Knot will be formed very easily.

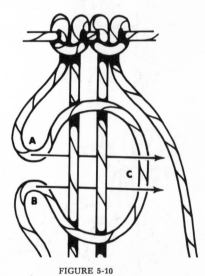

FIGURE 5-10

The Square Knot is more versatile than the Half Knot, and it occurs in many combinations in macramé. We will try some of these combinations in the next sample, but we will begin by learning the other basic knot of macramé, the Double Half Hitch.

FIGURE 5-11

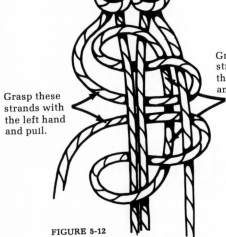

Grasp these
strands with
the left hand
and pull.

Grasp these
strands with
the right hand
and pull.

FIGURE 5-12

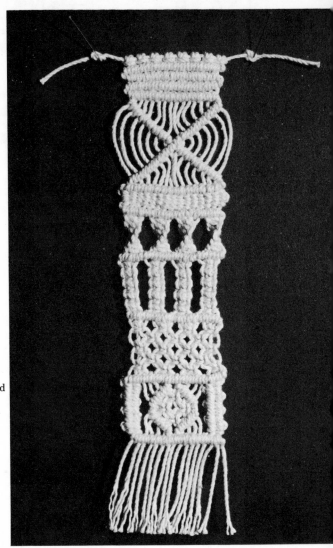

The completed sampler.

FIGURE 5-15

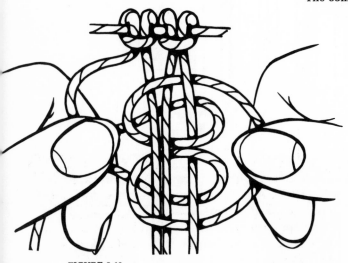

FIGURE 5-13

FIGURE 5-14

58

DIRECTIONS FOR A SAMPLER WITH THE DOUBLE HALF HITCH, THE HALF KNOT, AND THE SQUARE KNOT (FIG. 5-15)

The next piece is a sampler that is divided into seven sections. Only the Half Knot and the Square Knot, which you have learned, and the Double Half Hitch will be used. The sections are planned to show you some of the ways these knots can be used. Again, the measured lengths of the cords should be sufficient to complete the sampler if you follow the directions carefully and knot firmly.

Cut seven strands of Mason line 72 inches long.

Cut one strand of Mason line 116 inches long for the left-hand cord.

Cut one strand of Mason line 6 inches long for the holding cord.

The first eight cords are knotted on the holding cord with Reversed Double Half Hitches, the same way the previous samples were prepared for knotting (Fig. 5-16). All except the left-hand cord are doubled so they are 36 inches long. The left-hand cord is folded so that the outside cord —

cord 1 — measures 80 inches; cord 2, which is the other end of the doubled cord, thus measures 36 inches, or the same as the rest of the cords.

Horizontal Double Half Hitch:

We will start this sampler with the Double Half Hitch. For the first four rows we will knot Horizontal Double Half Hitches. Beginning at the right side, the first cord — cord 16 — will be used to knot over; it is called the *knot-bearer*. It is held in the left hand, *over the top of the other cords, and it is kept taut at all times* (Fig. 5-17). If the knot-bearing cord is not held taut, the knotting cord will not loop around it, and the work will not be correct.

With the right hand, pick up cord 15 and loop it toward the left hand in a clockwise direction; then it goes behind the knot-bearing cord and down in front of the loop (Fig. 5-18). Tighten firmly — *and remember to keep the knot-bearing cord taut.* This loop is repeated a second time with the same cord, thus forming the Double Half Hitch (Fig. 5-19). The same two loops are next knotted with cord 14, and then with

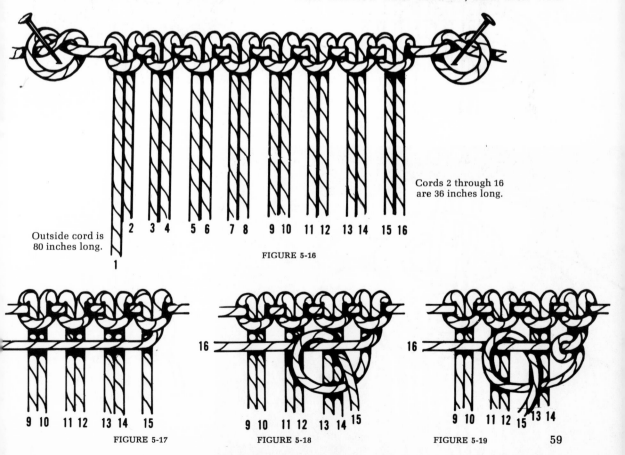

Cords 2 through 16 are 36 inches long.

Outside cord is 80 inches long.

2 3 4 5 6 7 8 9 10 11 12 13 14 15 16

1

FIGURE 5-16

16

9 10 11 12 13 14 15

FIGURE 5-17

16

9 10 11 12 13 14 15

FIGURE 5-18

9 10 11 12 15 13 14

FIGURE 5-19

59

each cord in succession across the row. *Do not forget that two loops are tied with each strand to form the Double Half Hitch.*

Since it is also necessary to make Double Half Hitches from left to right, we will turn around and go back with the same knots. Place a pin at the edge of the work just below the knot-bearing cord and reverse the direction of the cord around the pin (Fig. 5-20). Now the knot-bearing cord is held in the right hand *over the other cords and kept taut,* as before. With the left hand, pick up cord 1 and loop it toward the right hand in a counterclockwise direction; then it goes behind the knot-bearing cord and down in front of the loop (Fig. 5-21). Tighten firmly, again remembering to keep the knot-bearing cord taut. Tie a second loop in exactly the same way with the same cord. Now knot each successive cord in the same way from cord 2 through cord 15.

These Double Half Hitches are the same as those in the previous row, but you are progressing from left to right instead of from right to left as you did in the first row.

Fasten a pin at the right edge of the knots and reverse the direction of the knot-bearing cord just as you did at the left edge for the last row. Knot another row of Double Half Hitches from right to left; then reverse the knot-bearing cord around a pin again, and knot another row from left to right. This completes four rows of Horizontal Double Half Hitches (Fig. 5-22).

At first you may have some trouble keeping the rows of knots horizontal. This is controlled partly by the position in which you hold the knot-bearing cord. Sometimes it helps to hold the knot in place with the thumbnail of the hand that is holding the knot-bearing cord. Practice will teach you the best way.

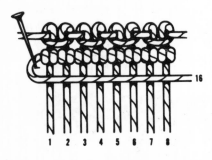

FIGURE 5-20

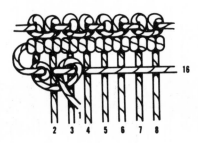

FIGURE 5-21

FIGURE 5-22

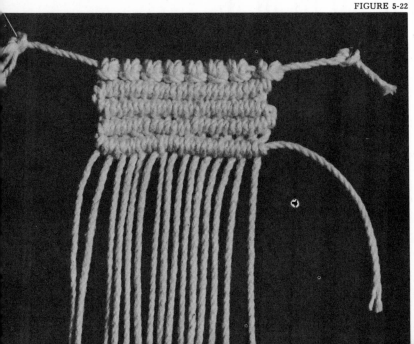

The first section of the sampler.

Diagonal Double Half Hitch:

The only difference between the Horizontal Double Half Hitch and the Diagonal Double Half Hitch is the position in which the knot-bearing cord is held as the knotting is done. In the second section of the sampler an X is made with the Diagonal Double Half Hitch.

Divide your cords into two groups of eight. Cord 1 becomes the knot-bearer, and it is held in the right hand at a 45-degree angle to the last row of knots. *It is kept taut at all times.* Cords 2, 3, 4, 5, 6, 7, and 8 are tied in Double Half Hitches over cord 1, which is kept at a 45-degree angle as each cord is knotted over it (Fig. 5-23).

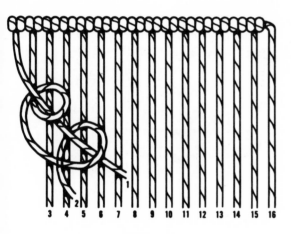

FIGURE 5-23

In the second group of eight cords, cord 16 becomes the knot-bearer, and it is held in the left hand at a 45-degree angle. Cords 15, 14, 13, 12, 11, 10, and 9 are knotted over it, in that order, in Double Half Hitches (Fig. 5-24).

Now we come to the intersection of the two knot-bearing cords, 1 and 16. They must be knotted together, and cord 16 becomes the knot-bearer. It is placed over cord 1 and held taut with the left hand. A Double Half Hitch is tied with cord 1 on cord 16 (Fig. 5-25).

The lower part of the X is completed by tying Double Half Hitches with cords 8, 7,

6, 5, 4, 3, and 2, in that order, over knot-bearing cord 16, which is held at a 45-degree angle. Cords 9, 10, 11, 12, 13, 14, and 15 are tied over knot-bearing cord 1, which is also held at a 45-degree angle. This completes the X (Fig. 5-26).

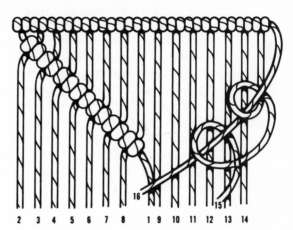

FIGURE 5-24

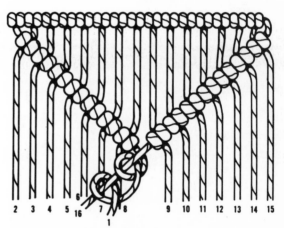

FIGURE 5-25

FIGURE 5-26

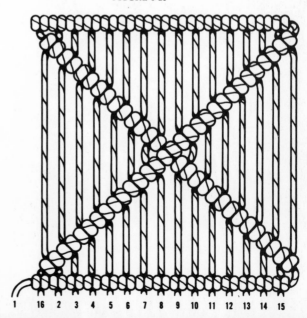

To separate this section of the sampler from the next, a row of Horizontal Double Half Hitches is knotted. Cord 1, which is at the right-hand edge of the sampler, is used as the knot-bearing cord, so place a pin at that edge. Place cord 1 over the top of the rest of the cords, hold it taut, and knot a row of Horizontal Double Half Hitches over it. (It is important that cord 1 is used as the knot-bearing cord for this row because it is the long cord that will be used to tie all the Vertical Double Half Hitches in the next section of the sampler.) Fig. 5-27 shows the sampler completed this far. We are ready to start the Vertical Double Half Hitches.

Vertical Double Half Hitch:

To keep the directions simple, we will renumber the cords 1 through 16 from left to right.

In all of the Double Half Hitches we have knotted so far, the knot-bearing cord remains the same across a row or down a diagonal, while the knotting cords change with the completion of each knot. The process reverses in the Vertical Double Half Hitch. The knot-bearing cord changes at the completion of each knot, and the knotting cord remains the same.

We will knot the first row from left to right, so place a pin on the left side of the sampler and reverse the direction of cord 1 around it. Cord 1 will be the knotting cord, and at the beginning of the knot it must lie under cord 2 (Fig. 5-28). Cord 2 is the knot-bearer, so it must be held taut in the left hand while you knot with cord 1. Using the right hand, loop cord 1 to the left, clockwise; it goes behind the knot-bearing cord and down in front of the loop. Tighten it firmly, keeping the knot-bearing cord taut. Repeat the loop a second time and tighten firmly. This completes the Vertical Double Half Hitch (Fig. 5-29).

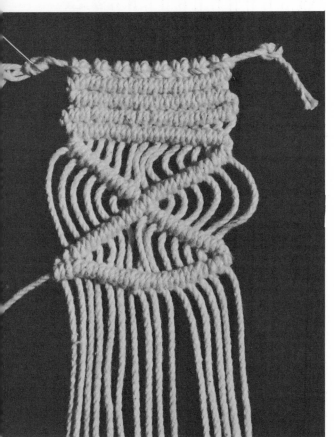

FIGURE 5-27

The first two sections of the sampler.

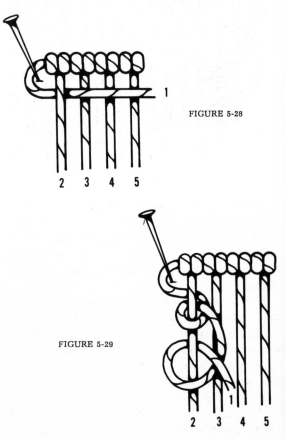

1

FIGURE 5-28

2   3   4   5

FIGURE 5-29

1

2   3   4   5

Now cord 1 is placed under cord 3, which becomes the next knot-bearing cord, and cord 1 is knotted over cord 3 just as it was knotted over cord 2. This same process is repeated across the row, with 4, 5, 6, and each successive cord becoming the knot-bearer in its turn (Fig. 5-30). Each time you pick up a new knot-bearing cord and start a new knot, the first loop of the knotting cord must be tightened very firmly because the knots should lie as close together as possible. As you tighten each loop, *remember to keep the knot-bearer taut.*

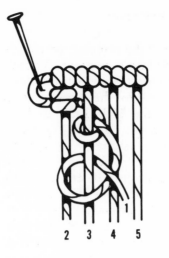

FIGURE 5-30

When the row is completed, and cord 16 is knotted over, place a pin at the right side of the work and reverse the direction of knotting cord 1 around it. Vertical Double Half Hitches are knotted across the cords from right to left by reversing the order of knotting and the knotting process. Cord 16 becomes the first knot-bearer; it is held taut in the right hand while the knotting cord is looped in a counterclockwise direction with the left hand (Fig. 5-31). *Remember to place the knotting cord under the knot-bearing cord before each knot is started.* Cords 15, 14, 13, etc. become knot-bearers as the knotting proceeds across the row.

FIGURE 5-31

You will note that the Vertical Double Half Hitch consumes the knotting yarn very rapidly, so if you are planning to knot a piece that has Vertical Double Half Hitches, your strands should be longer than the length calculated for other knots. That is why the directions for this sampler require extra length for cord 1.

Even if your knots are tightened firmly, you may notice some distortion in the section of Vertical Double Half Hitches. The separation bar of Horizontal Double Half Hitches to be knotted next will reduce this distortion and serve to divide the section of Vertical Double Half Hitches from the next section of the sampler. A pin is placed at the left side of the work and cord 1 is reversed around it, becoming the knot-bearer for a row of Horizontal Double Half Hitches knotted from left to right (Fig. 5-32).

FIGURE 5-32

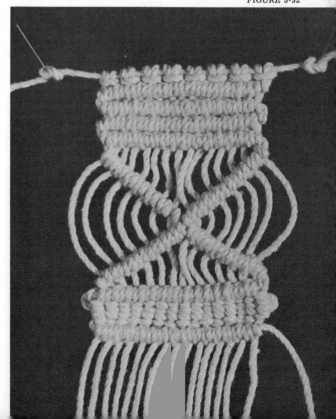

Half Knot:

For this section of the sampler, we divide the sixteen strands into four groups of four strands each and knot a short spiral sinnet with each group. Follow the directions on page 56 for tying the Half Knot and tie seven Half Knots in each group (Fig. 5-33).

Now knot another separator by placing a pin at the right side, reversing the last strand on the right around it, and knotting a row of Horizontal Double Half Hitches. You must watch the strands carefully to keep them in order as you knot this row. The strands that come from a row of Half Knots or Square Knots do not lie in order as neatly as those from a row of Double Half Hitches.

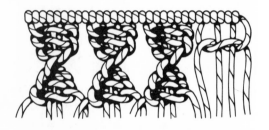

FIGURE 5-33

Figure 5-34 shows the sampler completed this far.

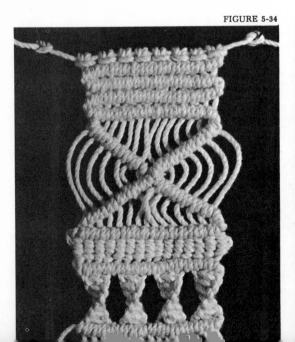

FIGURE 5-34

Square Knot:

For this section the strands of the sampler are again divided into four groups of four strands each. Each of the groups is knotted with five consecutive Square Knots, like those in the Square Knot sinnet described above on page 56 (Fig. 5-35).

Now knot another separator by placing a pin at the left side, reversing the last strand on the left around it, and knotting a row of Horizontal Double Half Hitches (Fig. 5-36).

The sixth section is also knotted with the Square Knot, but the knots are arranged alternately. To simplify the explanation, the cords will again be renumbered 1 through 16 from left to right. Again divide the strands into four groups of four strands each and knot one Square Knot in each group. As illustrated in Fig. 5-37, cords 1, 2, 3, and 4 are the first group; 5, 6, 7, and 8, the second group; 9, 10, 11, and 12, the

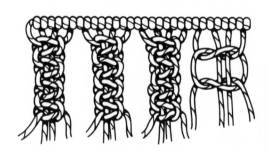

FIGURE 5-35

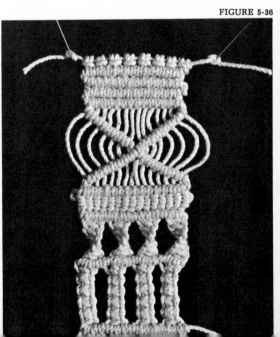

FIGURE 5-36

rows give you a small sample of the pattern that is created by knotting the Square Knot in alternate arrangement.

Now we are ready to knot another separator. Place a pin at the right edge, reverse the last strand around it, and knot a row of Horizontal Double Half Hitches (Fig. 5-40).

Row 1. →

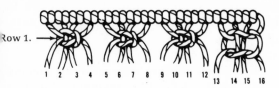

FIGURE 5-37

Row 1. →
Row 2. →

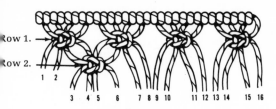

FIGURE 5-38

third group; and *13, 14, 15,* and *16,* the fourth group. In the second row of knots cords *1* and *2* are left inactive, and *3, 4, 5,* and *6* are knotted together in a Square Knot. The next two groups — cords *7, 8, 9,* and *10,* and *11, 12, 13,* and *14* — are successively knotted; cords *15* and *16* are left inactive (Fig. 5-38). The third row is knotted exactly like the first row, the fourth row like the second row, and the fifth row like the first row (Fig. 5-39). These five

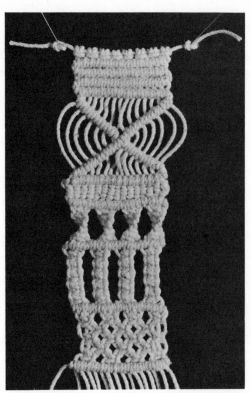

FIGURE 5-40

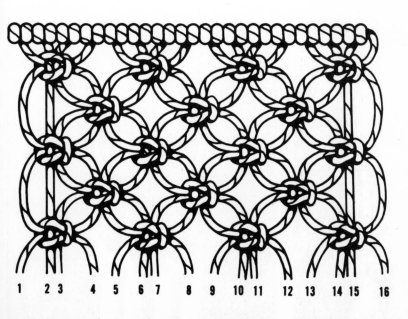

FIGURE 5-39

Combining the Double Half Hitch and the Square Knot in a Pattern:

The last section of the sampler will show you one way a design can be made: we will combine the knots you learned in the previous sections of the sampler. Cords 1, 2, and 3 on the left and 14, 15, and 16 on the right will be made into vertical borders after we have finished a diamond design in the center. Leave the border strands inactive and divide the ten remaining strands into two groups of five strands each, with 4, 5, 6, 7, and 8 forming one group and 9, 10, 11, 12, and 13 forming the other group (Fig. 5-41). Using cord 8 as a knot-bearing cord held at a 45-degree angle, knot cords 7, 6, 5, and 4 over it, in that order, in Diagonal Double Half Hitches. Then pick up cord 9 and, using it as a knot-bearer held at the opposite 45-degree angle, knot cords 10, 11, 12, and 13 over it in Diagonal Double Half Hitches, so the two knot-bearing cords form the top half of a diamond or lozenge shape (Fig. 5-42).

Place a pin at the end of both of the knotted rows of Diagonal Double Half Hitches. These will be used to turn the knot-bearing cord on when you complete the diamond.

The center of the diamond shape is knotted with the Square Knot in alternate arrangement (Figs. 5-7 through 5-14; 5-37, 5-38, and 5-39). The first knot is tied with cords 6, 7, 10, and 11 (Fig. 5-42). Cords 4, 5, 6, and 7 are knotted next, and cords 10, 11, 12, and 13 make a third Square Knot (Fig. 5-43). The last Square Knot, at the bottom of the diamond, is knotted with cords 6, 7, 10, and 11 again.

To complete the diamond, bend knot-bearing cord 8 around the pin placed at the left corner of the diamond and knot cords 4, 5, 6, and 7 in the Diagonal Double Half Hitch. Knot-bearing cord 9 is bent around the pin at the right side of the diamond, and cords 13, 12, 11, and 10 are knotted, in that order, to complete the diamond (Fig. 5-44).

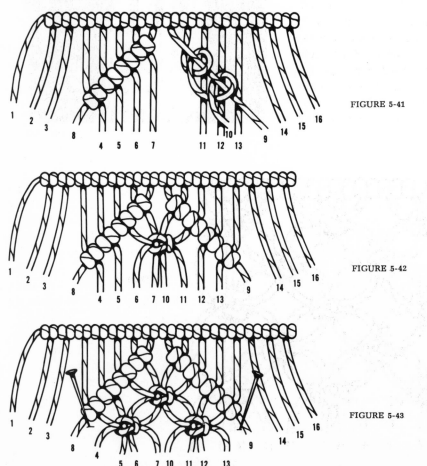

FIGURE 5-41

FIGURE 5-42

FIGURE 5-43

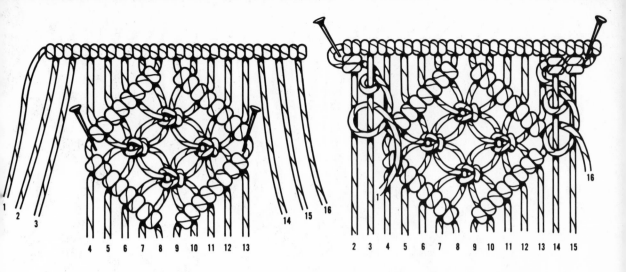

FIGURE 5-44

FIGURE 5-45

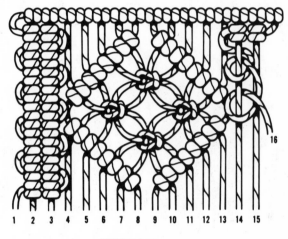

FIGURE 5-46

Now we are ready to knot cords *1*, *2*, and *3* and *14*, *15*, and *16*, to finish this section of the sampler with vertical borders. These borders will be knotted with the Vertical Double Half Hitch. In the group on the left side, cord *1* is the knotting cord and cords *2* and *3* are the knot-bearers. Cord *1* is placed under cord *2*, and a Vertical Double Half Hitch is tied (Figs. 5-28, 5-29, and 5-45). Then cord *1* is placed under cord *3*, and another Vertical Double Half Hitch is tied. Now we turn the knotting cord and knot from right to left (Figs. 5-31 and 5-45) using cord *3* as a knot-bearer again. Cord *2* is the next strand used as knot-bearer, and

this order is continued: *2* and *3*, knotting from left to right; then *3* and *2*, knotting from right to left; *2* and *3* from left to right again; *3* and *2* from right to left again, until the knotted border is as long as the diamond (Fig. 5-46). The right border is then completed in the same manner, using cord *16* as the knotting cord and cords *14* and *15* as the knot-bearers.

To complete your sampler, place a pin at the left side, reverse the last strand on the left around it, and knot one more row of Horizontal Double Half Hitches. The remaining cords can be trimmed and left as a fringe.

67

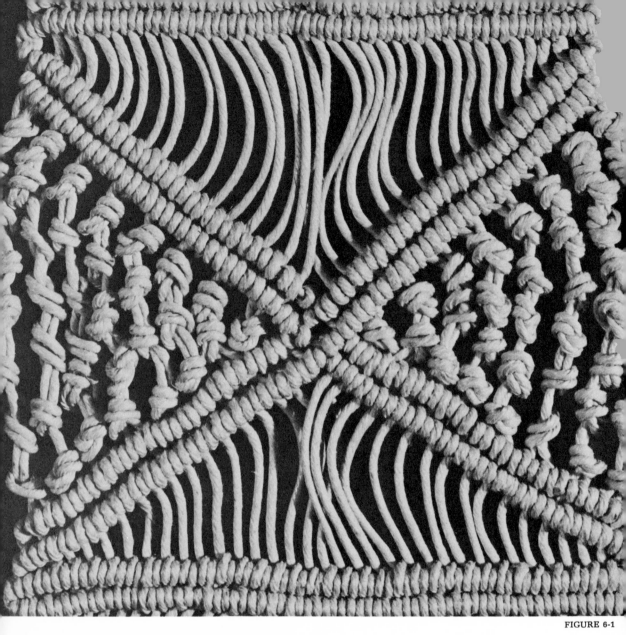

FIGURE 6-1

The Overhand Knot tied in double strands in an X motif.

This attractive border is knotted with groups of four cords. In each group a Square Knot is tied first, then an Overhand Knot is tied in the two center cords, and another Square Knot completes the pattern.

FIGURE 6-2

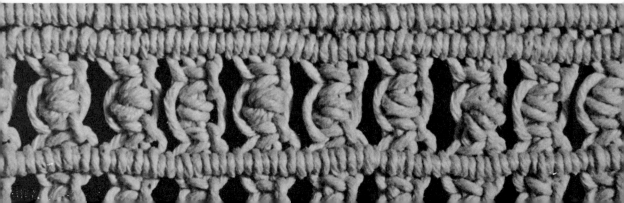

6

OTHER KNOTS

Overhand Knot

There are a few other knots that are used occasionally in macramé. One of them is the Overhand Knot, which was introduced to you as a knot for holding your work on the knotting base (see Figs. 4-7, 4-8, and 4-9). This simple little knot has many other uses, and it can be varied in several ways: the Overhand Knot tied in a single strand (Fig. 6-3); the Overhand Knot tied in a double strand (Fig. 6-4), and the Overhand Knot tied over a strand (Fig. 6-5). The borders of the *rebozo* shown in Figs. 6-6 and 6-7 were knotted entirely in the Overhand Knot.

The Overhand Knot was used in a very ingenious way on a sash from Mexico (Figs. 6-8 and 6-9). Red and white warp yarns were used in the woven pattern in the sash, and both of these colors form the fringe. The Overhand Knot tied over a strand was used. Each knot contains a red and a white yarn (Fig. 6-10A), and the color that shows in the knotted area is controlled by the strand that is knotted. If a white knot is needed in the pattern, the white yarn is knotted over the red yarn (Figs. 6-10B and 6-10C). If the pattern calls for a red knot, the red yarn is knotted over the white yarn (Figs. 6-10D and 6-10E). These knots are tied adjacent to one another so none of the knotting cords can be seen between them.

FIGURE 6-3

FIGURE 6-4

FIGURE 6-5

FIGURE 6-6

The knotted fringe of a cotton *rebozo* from northern Peru. Both ends of the garment have this knotted design. The knotted areas measure 17½ by 27½ inches. (Given to the author for her collection by Grace G. Denny)

FIGURE 6-7

Detail from Fig. 6-6.

FIGURE 6-8

A Mexican sash with part of the fringe knotted in a simple geometric design. (Given to the author for her collection by Nathallie Fitzgerald)

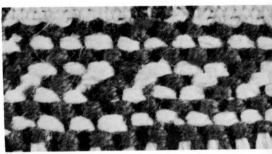

Detail from Fig. 6-8.

FIGURE 6-9

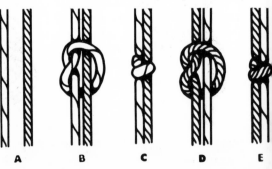

A   B   C   D   E

FIGURE 6-10

Josephine Knot

The Josephine Knot is an interwoven knot that is also known as a "Carrick Bend" (Fig. 6-16). Although the knot is not difficult to tie, a written description becomes quite involved. The first few times you tie it you will need to follow the diagrams carefully.

Cut two lengths of cord, each about 8 inches long. (One dark and one light colored cord are used in the diagrams to make them easier to understand.) Holding cord A-B in the left hand, make a loop in it, as in Fig. 6-11, so end A points toward you, end B points away from you, and end A rests on top of end B. Place the second cord, C-D, diagonally under the loop (Fig. 6-12) so end C is at the upper right and end D is at the lower left of the loop. Ends A, B, and C remain in this position, and end D is interwoven with the other ends to form the knot. Take end D and curve it upward and to the left, placing it over cord A-B near end A, as in Fig. 6-13. Next, end D goes under cord A-B near end B (Fig. 6-14); it passes down over the loop diagonally, going over cord A-B, under cord C-D, and over cord A-B again (Fig. 6-15).

If you have been able to follow these involved directions — congratulations! It is an attractive knot, isn't it? It can be tightened firmly or not, depending upon the effect you want to achieve. Pulling on ends A and B with one hand at the same time as you pull on ends C and D with the other hand will tighten the knot. The interlacement of yarns shows more clearly when the knot is not tightened firmly; however, the tightened knot becomes an attractive oval-shaped form that can be introduced in many places in your knotting.

If two or more strands are used for each cord, they will form a larger, flatter knot that is also attractive. Two strands were used in the braid in Fig. 6-16 and the wall hanging in Fig. 6-17. In the braid every

other knot was reversed to keep the braid from twisting. The reversed knot is tied in exactly the same way, except that you start with a loop in the right-hand cord, and the left-hand cord is interwoven into it — just the reverse of the directions given above.

If you find this difficult to visualize, place a mirror at a right angle to Figs. 6-11 through 6-15 to reverse the diagrams.

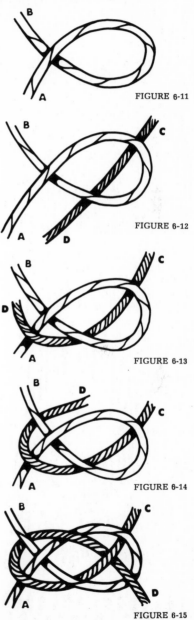

FIGURE 6-11

FIGURE 6-12

FIGURE 6-13

FIGURE 6-14

FIGURE 6-15

Josephine Knots tied with two strands of size 12/18 linen cord.

FIGURE 6-16

Josephine Knots are used in the design of this wall
hanging knotted by Betty Lu Kulp.

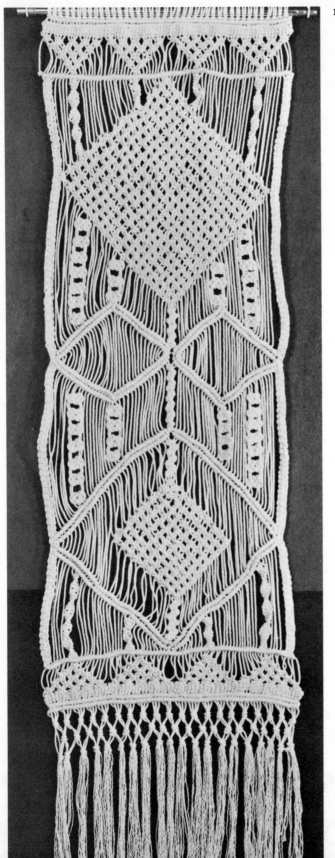

FIGURE 6-17

FIGURE 6-18

FIGURE 6-19

Half Hitch

The variety of effects that can be achieved with the simple little loop that forms the Half Hitch is almost infinite. It is looped in different directions and in different combinations to form knots that are known by other names.

When cords are looped alternately over each other they are known as chains or, sometimes, bars (Fig. 6-20). Two cords will make a single chain (Fig. 6-18), and four cords will make a double chain (Fig. 6-19). A single chain is begun, as illustrated in Fig. 6-21, by holding cord 1 taut with the left hand while, with the right hand, cord 2 is curved over cord 1 and looped around under it. Now the end of cord 2 is brought back between the two cords and down over the curve of cord 2.

The next loop is the exact reverse (Fig. 6-22). Cord 2 is held taut. Cord 1 is curved over it, looped around and under it, and brought back between the two cords. The two loops are repeated alternately to form the chain. (In Fig. 7-27 there is a row each of single and double chains, and chains are also used in Figs. 7-29 and 8-6.)

Variations can be made by looping one cord more than once before changing to the alternate cord. It is fun to try different combinations, such as two loops on one side, then one on the other, or two on each side.

A series of Half Hitches can be tied over a cord that acts only as a knot-bearing cord, or core (Fig. 6-23). This form of knotting was used to make the design between the arms of the X in Fig. 6-24. It can also be used to form an interesting checkerboard pattern (see Fig. 7-33).

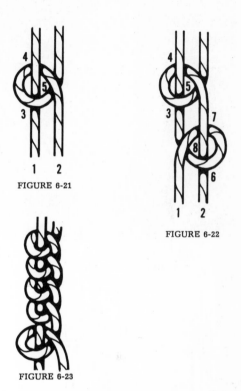

FIGURE 6-21

FIGURE 6-22

FIGURE 6-23

Chains with two, four, and six cords are tied in this X motif.

FIGURE 6-20

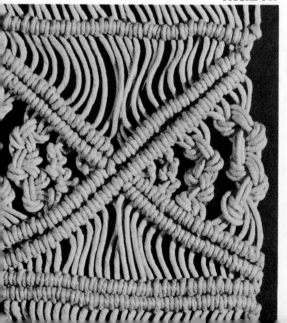

Half Hitches are tied over a core of two cords in this X motif.

FIGURE 6-24

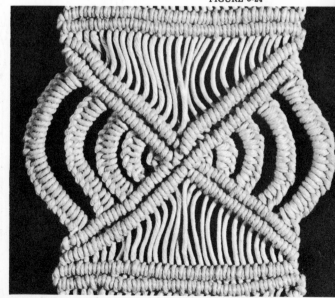

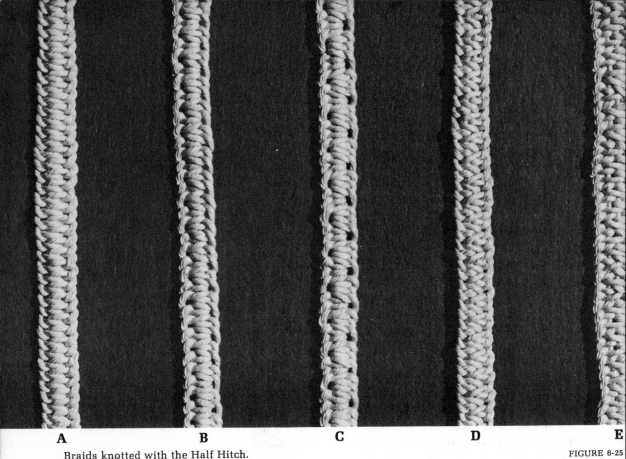

A   **B**   **C**   **D**   **E**

Braids knotted with the Half Hitch.

FIGURE 6-25

FIGURE 6-26

FIGURE 6-27

FIGURE 6-28

1   2   3   4

FIGURE 6-29

1   2   3   4

FIGURE 6-30

Many braids can be tied with the Half Hitch. Usually four cords are used — two center cords for the core and two outer cords that are knotted on the core alternately in single Half Hitches or in groups of Half Hitches. Fig. 6-25 shows a few examples of these braids, and they are knotted as follows:

A The right-hand cord is tied in a Half Hitch over the center two cords; then the left-hand cord is Half Hitched over the center two cords. Continue to tie alternately (Fig. 6-26).

B The right-hand cord is tied in two Half Hitches over the center cords; then the same two knots are tied with the left-hand cord over the center cords. Repeat (Fig. 6-27).

C This braid is the same as *A* and *B* except that three Half Hitches are tied instead of one or two (Fig. 6-28).

D The right-hand cord (cord 4) is tied in a Half Hitch over cord 3; then this same cord is tied in a Half Hitch over cords 2 and 3 together. The left-hand cord (cord 1) is tied in the same sequence — first over cord 2, then over 2 and 3 together. Repeat (Fig. 6-29).

E The right-hand cord (cord 4) is tied in a Half Hitch, first over cord 3, then over 2 and 3 together, then over 3 again. The left-hand cord is tied in the same sequence — first over 2, then 2 and 3 together, then 2 again. Repeat from the beginning (Fig. 6-30).

An X motif using Reversed Double Half Hitches tied over a core of two cords. Compare Figs. 6-20 and 6-24.

Reversed Double Half Hitch

If you change the direction of the next loop after you have made one Half Hitch, you will make the Reversed Double Half Hitch. As illustrated in Fig. 6-31, the first loop is a Half Hitch. The second loop goes under the core or knot-bearing cord, around and over it horizontally. Then the end goes back, into the space between the two cords and down under the cord leading from the first Half Hitch. The two loops form the Reversed Double Half Hitch laid on its side.

FIGURE 6-31

This knot, like the Half Hitch, can be used in many combinations to make a variety of braids, and a few of these are illustrated in Fig. 6-33. To make these braids, you knot as follows:

FIGURE 6-32

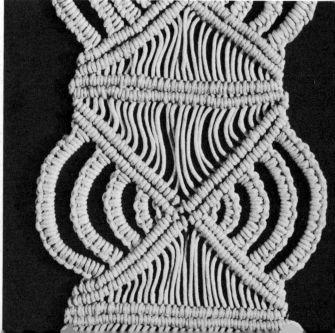

A   B   C   D

Braids knotted with the Reversed Double Half Hitch.

FIGURE 6-34

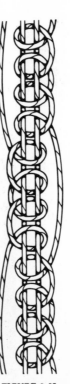

FIGURE 6-35

1   2   3   4   5   6   7   8

FIGURE 6-36

A The right-hand cord is tied in the Reversed Double Half Hitch over the center two cords; then the left-hand cord is tied in the Reversed Half Hitch over the center two cords. Continue to alternate these knots (Fig. 6-34).

B The right-hand cord is tied in two Reversed Double Half Hitches over the center cords; then the left-hand cord is tied in the same two knots over the center cords. Repeat (Fig. 6-35).

C This braid is tied exactly like braid B except that each knot is spaced a short distance away from the preceding knot, tightened firmly, and then pushed up next to the preceding knot. This forms the loops between the knots, and the amount of cord left between the knots when they are tied controls the size of the loops that extend out from the braid.

D This braid is the same as A except that it is doubled — eight cords are used instead of four. Cords 2 and 3 are the center cords for one half of the braid; cords 6 and 7 are the center cords for the other

half. The two braids are knotted simultaneously, in the same order as braid A. Cords 4 and 5 are crossed between the Reversed Double Half Hitches to unite the two braids (Fig. 6-36).

Very different effects can be achieved if you use more than one color for knotting braids. One dark and one light outside cord are used in the braids in Fig. 6-37. Varying the texture of the yarns within a braid also changes its appearance, and more than one size of yarn might give it quite a different quality.

Fig. 6-32 shows yet another version of the X motif used in Figs. 6-1, 6-20, and 6-24. Here the cords between the arms of the X have been knotted with Reversed Double Half Hitches. The possible variations in knotting are unlimited, and it is fun to try different combinations.

When the Half Hitch or the Reversed Double Half Hitch is knotted over a core of several cords, an open space is left around the knots. Thus, these knots are useful in many designs to create a pleasant contrast of positive-negative space.

Braids knotted with two colors. A is the same as A in Fig. 6-25, B is the same as D in Fig. 6-25, C is the same as E in Fig. 6-25, and D is the same as A in Fig. 6-33.

FIGURE 6-37

A

B

C

D

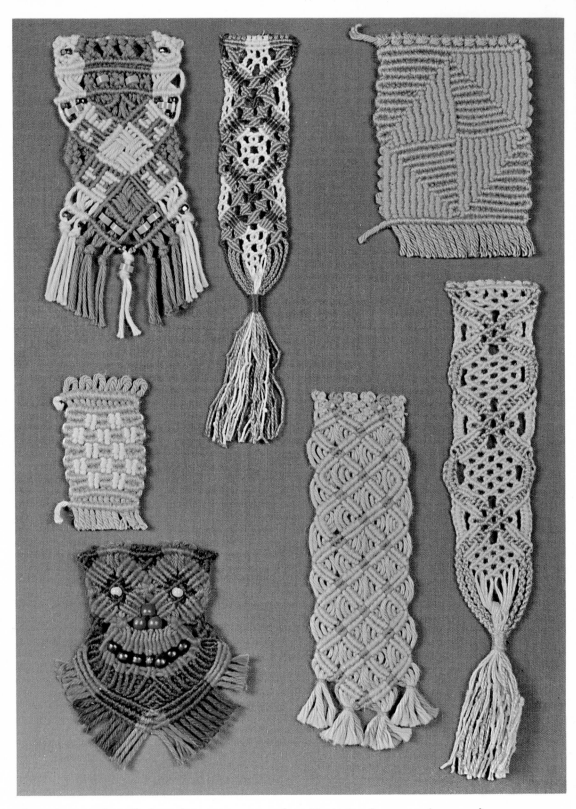

This selection of small pieces in two or more colors illustrates the way colors can be controlled to appear and disappear in a knotted design. The brown, tan, and cream piece and the grey and yellow piece are bookmarks that were knotted by Ada Treves Segre.

The design at the hem of this velvet evening skirt was assembled from knotted braids and small pieces of macramé attached to the background with decorative stitchery. The turquoise and khaki green pieces are silk, and the acid yellow and white braids are wool. Stitches taken from *The Stitches of Creative Embroidery* by Jacqueline Enthoven were used between the braids and around the blue green pieces to attach them to the velvet.

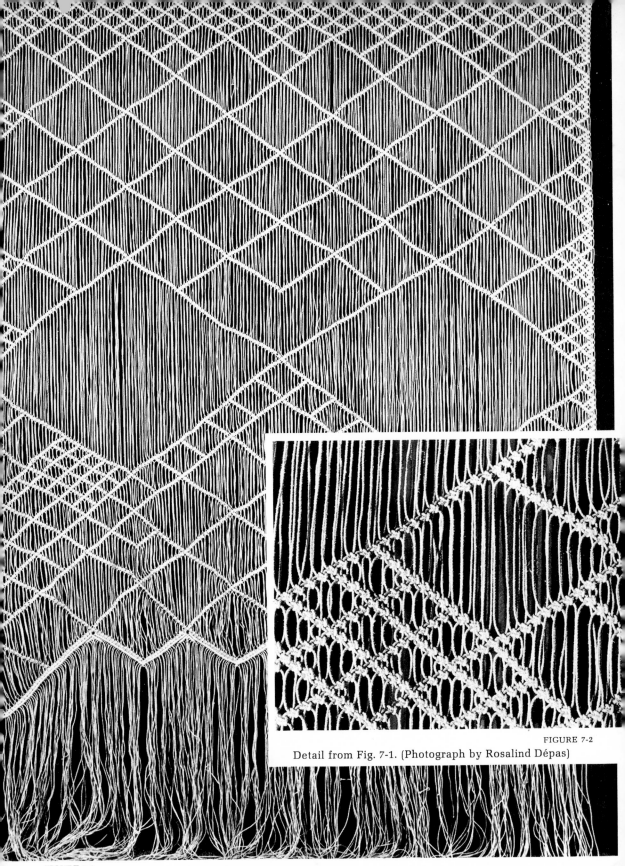

FIGURE 7-2

Detail from Fig. 7-1. (Photograph by Rosalind Dépas)

FIGURE 7-1

A wall hanging knotted with diagonal lines of Square Knots by Spencer Dépas. 8 by 10 feet. (Photograph by Monika Reichelt)

7

DESIGN AND COLOR IN MACRAME

Knotters of the past have combined the knots of macramé in many patterns. The variety of these patterns is a tribute to the imagination of man, particularly when you realize that most of the designs use only two knots, the Square Knot and the Double Half Hitch. A few patterns and directions for them are illustrated and discussed in this chapter; any of these patterns can be used for knotting a project. However, I hope that you will study the way the knots combine to form pattern, and that the designs here will serve as an inspiration to help you design your own.

When you design with knotting, there are many elements to consider. The pattern of the piece as a whole is usually the first consideration. To achieve this pattern you should be concerned with the textural quality of the surface and the density of the design areas. The surface texture is determined by the combination of the material and the knotting pattern. There are a wide variety of patterns illustrated in this book, and a study of them should help you visualize the surface you need.

The density of the knotting is a major element in the interplay of surfaces in a design. If you compare the restrained geometric design of the large wall hanging in Figs. 7-1 and 7-2 with the small, varied, and richly ornamental piece in Fig. 7-18, you will see the variety of design that is possible. Unknotted areas are an important element in the large hanging, and this gives the piece a feeling of simplicity and freedom that is very pleasant. In comparison, the design of the small hanging is tight and dense, and it uses variety as a theme. However, unity has been achieved by the repetition of some of the elements, for example, the diamond and the X figures. The knotter was careful to balance the density of the areas even though they are varied. The piece is both playful and decorative.

The pattern in Fig. 7-19 depends upon an interplay of density and textural quality. The triangles of spiral sinnets are open areas in contrast to the medium density of the Square Knotted triangles and the dense Diagonal Half Hitched triangles. A very simple interplay of surfaces is employed in the design of the piece shown in Fig. 2-7. The contrast of open and dense areas in a design is particularly attractive when the piece is hung so that it is viewed with the light behind it.

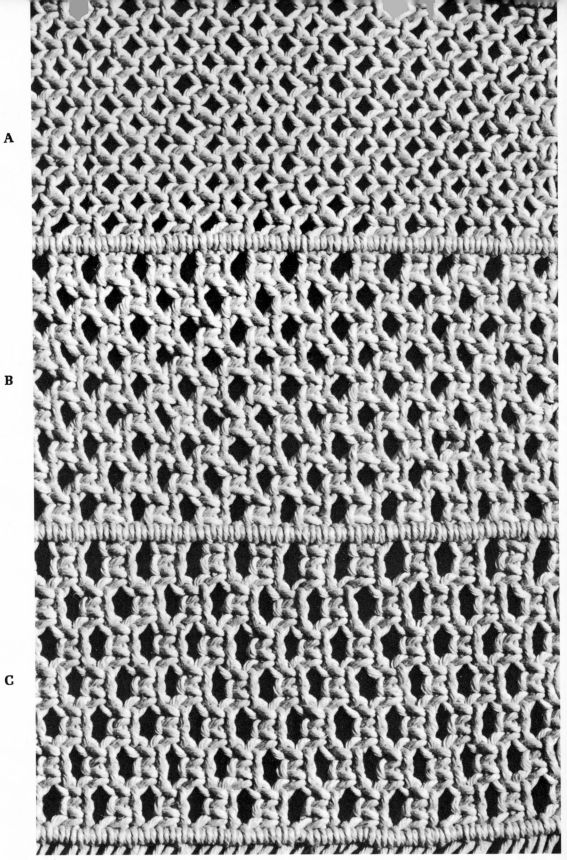

A

B

C

Patterns of Square Knots.

FIGURE 7-3

Patterns of Square Knots

Most of the patterns included in this chapter are rather firm, closely-knotted designs. The three patterns in Fig. 7-3 are repeat patterns forming an over-all design that becomes a textured surface in large areas. Each of these designs is knotted in the same sequence, but the change in surface texture and density is achieved by the difference in the knots. This difference is apparent when you compare the following directions for each section:

A In this pattern of Square Knots in alternate arrangement, the knots form diagonal rows that fit well in a design with diagonal lines. (See, for instance, Figs. 1-25 and 7-13.) In Fig. 7-4 the first row of knots and the first two knots of the second row have been tied, and the third knot of the second row is being tied. The following rows repeat rows 1 and 2, so row 3 will be the same as row 1; row 4 will be the same as row 2. This sequence is repeated until the desired area is knotted.

B This pattern illustrates the Square Knot plus the Half Knot (also known as a Triple Knot) in alternate arrangement. The design creates a regular pattern that is a little less dense than the one above. Since each knot is larger, steeper diagonal lines are formed. This pattern makes an attractive textured surface that will also fit into a design with diagonal lines. It is knotted in exactly the same sequence as the pattern above except that a Square Knot and a Half Knot, as shown in Fig. 7-5, are tied each time.

C Here two full Square Knots are tied alternately in rows to form a pattern with steeper diagonals and a more open effect than either of the previous designs. The sequence for tying the knots is the same as for patterns A and B (Fig. 7-6).

Graph paper can be used for planning repeat patterns of Square Knots. Alternate squares or vertical groups of alternate squares must be used, and each darkened square of the graph paper represents one Square Knot. For example, Fig. 7-9 is the plan for section A of Fig. 7-7.

FIGURE 7-4

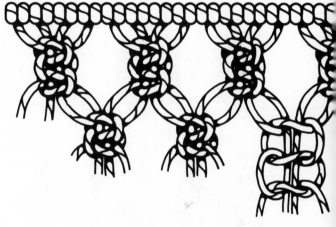

FIGURE 7-5

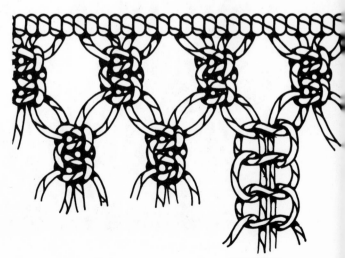

FIGURE 7-6

83

A

B

C

Patterns of Square Knots.

FIGURE 7-7

A In this pattern row 1 has three Square Knots tied in sequence in each group of four cords. Fig. 7-8 shows three groups of the first row of knots completed and the last knot in the fourth group being tied. Row 2 has one Square Knot tied in the alternate group of four cords and the third knot in this row is being tied. Row 3 repeats row 1; the last knot of the first group of this row is illustrated. Row 4 will repeat row 2.

B Fig. 7-10 is the plan on graph paper for section B of Fig. 7-7. Looking at Fig. 7-11, you will see that the first two rows of this pattern are exactly the same as the first two rows of pattern A. The third row has only one Square Knot in each alternate group, and then the fourth row repeats the four Square Knots like the first row, but these groups of knots are in the alternate position. Two more rows of single knots, then another row of four knots are tied to continue the pattern.

C To start the pattern in section C, the cords are divided into groups of six cords each (Fig. 7-12). Starting at either side and working with the first group of six cords, a Square Knot is tied in the center four cords of the group. The next Square Knot is tied with the two outside cords of the group, over the center four cords, and it is positioned just below the first knot. The third Square Knot is tied in the center four cords again. This same sequence of knots is followed in each group of six cords.

The second row is knotted in the same sequence, but alternate groups of six cords are used. The third row repeats the first row, the fourth row repeats the second row, etc.

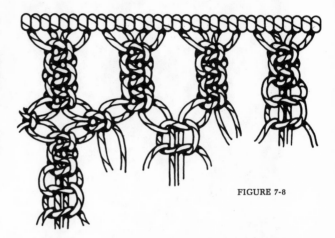

FIGURE 7-8

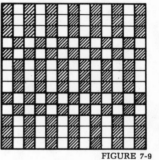

FIGURE 7-9

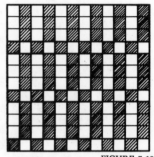

FIGURE 7-10

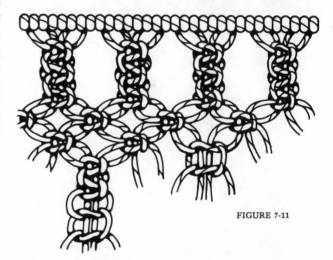

FIGURE 7-11

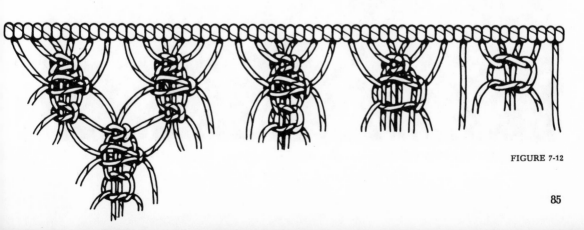

FIGURE 7-12

A

B

Double Half Hitches form the diagonal lines that are the basic element of these patterns.

FIGURE 7-13

Patterns of Double Half Hitches

Many of the patterns of macramé use more of the Double Half Hitch than the Square Knot. Section A of Fig. 7-13 shows a simple design based on the Diagonal Double Half Hitch, and section B illustrates various center designs in the diamond motif. A few of the other possible variations and combinations of the diamond motif are shown in Fig. 7-50.

A To knot this pattern, the cords are divided into groups of eight cords (Fig. 7-14). Cord 1 becomes the knot-bearing cord for a diagonal going from upper left to lower right. Cords 2, 3, and 4 are knotted with Double Half Hitches on cord 1. Cord 8 is used for the knot-bearing cord for the diagonal from upper right to lower left. Cords 7, 6, and 5 are knotted on it in succession. Cord 1 is then knotted on cord 8, thus completing the upper part of the X. Cords 4, 3, and 2 knotted in succession on cord 8 continue the right to left diagonal, and cords 5, 6, and 7 knotted on cord 1 continue the left to right diagonal, thus completing the X. Each group of eight cords is knotted the same way (Fig. 7-15). The X's are joined by knotting cord 1 of the left-hand group over cord 8 of the right-hand group. To continue the pattern, another row of X's is started immediately below the last row.

B In this section the diamonds are formed with two rows of Diagonal Double Half Hitches. Groups of sixteen cords are used, and Fig. 7-16 shows the order of knotting. The center cords in the first row of diamonds are gathered together by tying a Square Knot over them (Fig. 7-17). The diamonds in the second row are filled with Square Knots in alternate arrangement (Fig. 7-20), and the center cords in the last row are interwoven (Fig. 7-21).

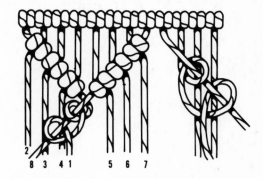

FIGURE 7-14

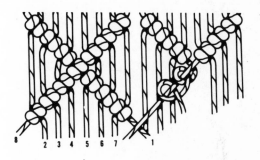

FIGURE 7-15

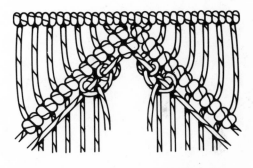

FIGURE 7-16

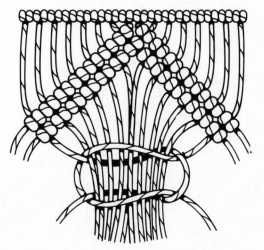

FIGURE 7-17

Very dark brown linen upholsterers' cord knotted in a variety of designs for a wall hanging. 8 by 10 inches.

FIGURE 7-18

The pattern in this fringe is sometimes called the "Japanese Pattern." (Courtesy of the Suffolk County Whaling Museum of Sag Harbor, Long Island. Photograph by Mel Jackson)

FIGURE 7-19

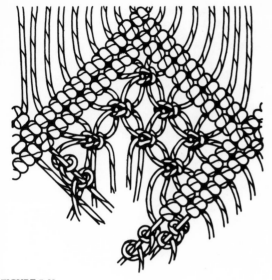

FIGURE 7-20

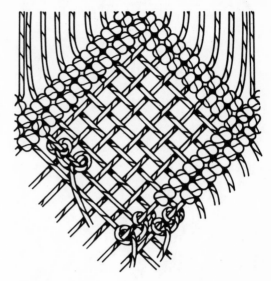

FIGURE 7-21

Curved lines knotted of Double Half Hitches form attractive designs in sections A and B of Fig. 7-22. Pattern C is the same as B except that the design is smaller in scale and the lines of Double Half Hitches have been knotted in a straight line instead of a curve.

A The secret of success in knotting this pattern is keeping an accurate count of the cords. The pattern is made with groups of eight cords (Fig. 7-23). The upper part of the leaf shape is made by knotting cords 7, 6, 5, 4, 3, 2, and 1 successively over cord 8, spacing the knots so the line forms a curve. Cord 7 becomes the knot-bearing cord for the lower part of the motif, and cords 6, 5, 4, 3, 2, 1, and 8 are knotted successively on it. These knots are also spaced in a curve to complete the leaf shape. This design is repeated in each group of eight cords.

For the second row (Fig. 7-24), cord 3 becomes the knot-bearing cord for the upper line of knotting. Cords 4, 5, and 6 of the first group of eight cords are knotted on cord 3. Then cords 7, 8, 1, and 2 of the second group of eight cords are knotted successively on cord 3. This completes the upper part of the leaf. For

the lower part, cord 4 of the first group of eight cords is used as the knot-bearing cord. Then cords 5 and 6 of the first group and 7, 8, 1, and 2 of the second group, and cord 3 of the first group (the knot-bearing cord for the upper part of the leaf) are knotted successively on cord 4 to complete the leaf. This design is repeated across the knotting.

The third row repeats the first row, and the fourth rows repeats the second row. It may help to separate the cords into the new groupings of eight cords that form the motifs before you start each row.

B The leaf motifs are arranged to form a new pattern as diagramed in Fig. 7-25. Groups of eight cords are used again. In the first group cords 2, 3, 4, 5, 6, 7, and 8 are knotted in turn on cord 1 for the upper line of knotting. The lower line is knotted with cords 3, 4, 5, 6, 7, 8, and 1 on cord 2. The second group uses cord 8 as the knot-bearing cord for the upper line, and cords 7, 6, 5, 4, 3, 2, and 1 are knotted on it, in that order. Cord 7 is the knot-bearing cord for the lower line, and cords 6, 5, 4, 3, 2, 1, and 8 are knotted on it. The two leaf forms are joined by knotting cord 2 of the first group over cord 7 of the second group. Cord 7 of

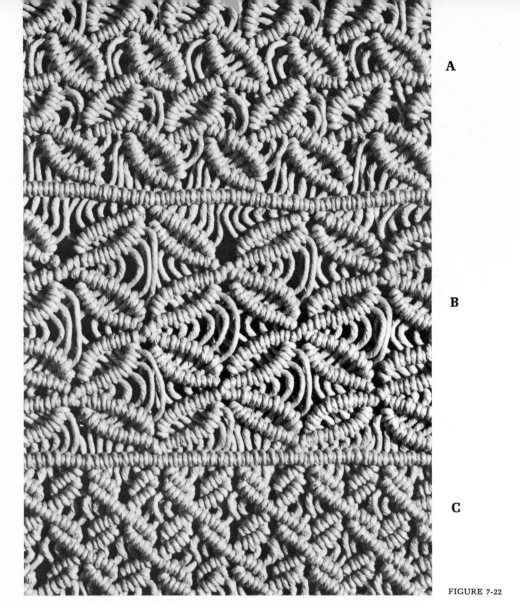

A

B

C

FIGURE 7-22

The leaf-shaped motifs in sections *A* and *B* are repeated to form over-all patterns. Section *C* is a variation of the pattern in section *B*.

the second group then becomes the knot-bearing cord for the upper part of the first leaf in the second row, and the other seven cords of the first group are knotted on it.

After cord 2 of the first group joins the two leaf shapes in the first row, it moves over into the second group of eight in the second row and becomes the knot-bearing cord for the upper part of the second leaf and the remaining seven cords of the second group are knotted on it. Row 3 repeats row 1, and row 4 repeats row 2.

C This pattern is a repeat of pattern *B* except that it is knotted in groups of four cords instead of groups of eight, and the Double Half Hitches are knotted in parallel diagonal lines instead of curves (Fig. 7-26).

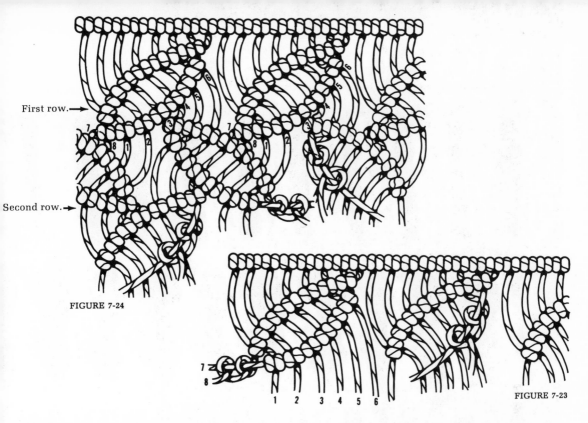

First row. →

Second row. →

FIGURE 7-24

FIGURE 7-23

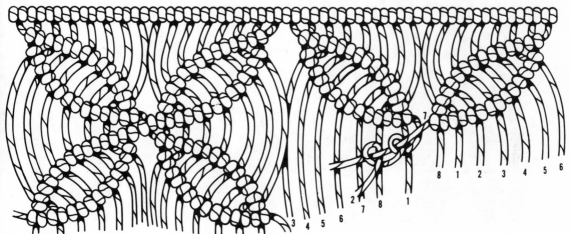

FIGURE 7-25

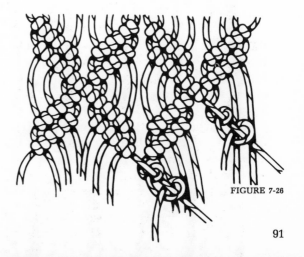

FIGURE 7-26

A

B

C

D

E

F

FIGURE 7-28

Bands of Vertical Stripes

Fig. 7-27 shows bands of design that are made by repeating vertical lines of knotting such as sinnets or chains side-by-side. The contrasts of density are very apparent, particularly between sections B and C. Thus, section B is very open, while section C is a solid, textured surface because the chains lie close together.

A The Square Knot is repeated in flat sinnets to make a pattern of vertical lines. Directions for the flat sinnet are given on page 56.

B Another pattern of vertical lines is knotted by repeating spiral sinnets. Directions for the spiral sinnet are given on page 55.

C Single chains knotted side-by-side fill the space completely and create a solid-looking textured surface. Directions for knotting the single chain are given on page 73.

D Repeating the double chain forms another pattern of vertical lines. Directions for this chain are given on page 73.

E Half Hitches are used to form this pattern. It is knotted by following the directions for the braid in Fig. 6-26.

F Half Hitches are used for this pattern also. To knot it follow the directions for the braid in Fig. 6-29 .

This detail of the wall-hanging in Fig. 8-44 combines bands of vertical stripes, square knot in an all-over pattern, and diamond motifs.

FIGURE 7-29

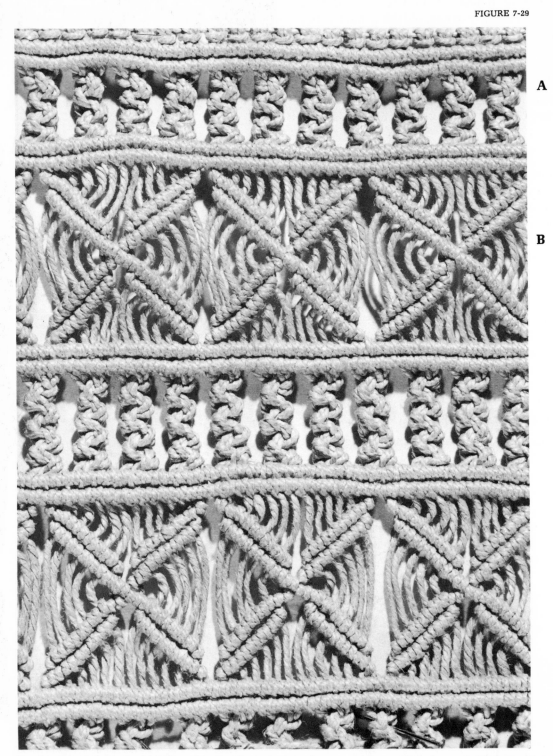

A

B

Bands of double chains and X motifs are alternated to form a pattern. (Courtesy of Edith L. Strand)

Attractive patterns can be formed by alternating bands of motifs. The design shown in Fig. 7-29 is pleasing partly because of the proportions of the bands and partly because of the contrast in pattern of the X's and the double chains.

A The double chain is repeated to make the first and third bands (Fig. 7-30).

B Each X motif is knotted with fourteen cords, seven on each side, as shown in Fig. 7-31. Except for the difference in the number of cords in each motif, the first line of Diagonal Double Half Hitches is knotted in the same way as the X in the sampler explained on page 61 to form the upper arms of the X. A second line of Diagonal Double Half Hitches is then knotted parallel and adjacent to the first row on each arm. Then the knot-bearing cord for the right-hand arm is knotted over the knot-bearing cord for the left-hand arm to unite the two arms. To complete the X, each of the lower arms is also knotted with two rows of Diagonal Double Half Hitches.

FIGURE 7-30

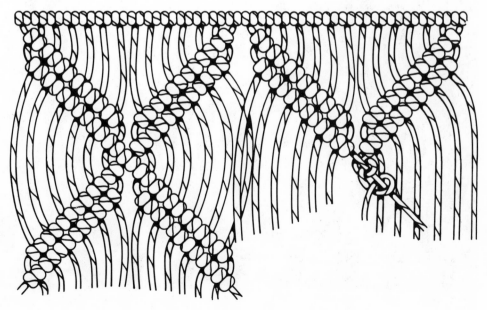

FIGURE 7-31

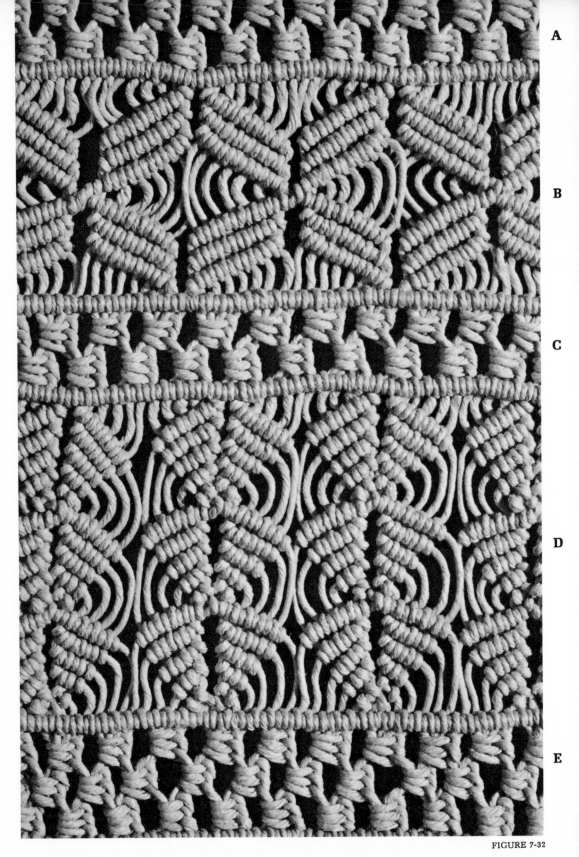

A

B

C

D

E

FIGURE 7-32

The bands of design used in this pattern are adapted from Fig. 1-4.

Patterns with Variety in Bands of Motifs

Bands of design are used again in Fig. 7-32. The success of the pattern is due, to a great extent, to the proportions of the bands and the repetition in the narrow bands. The bands are knotted as follows:

A As illustrated in Fig. 7-33, divide the cords into groups of four. Take the right-hand cord in each group (cord 4 in the first group) and tie three Half Hitches over the other three cords. When these knots are tied in each group across the knotting, the cords are regrouped. Two cords are taken from each of two adjacent groups — for instance, cords 3, 4, 5, and 6 are the first group in the second row of knots. The right-hand cord in the new group, cord 6, is then used to tie the three Half Hitches over the other three cords in this group.

B In this band of pattern, the X motif is knotted with three parallel rows of Diagonal Double Half Hitches. Each X is made with sixteen cords, eight on each side. Directions for knotting the arms of the X are the same as those given for the X in Fig. 7-31 except that three rows of Diagonal Double Half Hitches are used in each arm instead of two.

C This band is the same as section A.

D For this motif the cords are divided into groups of six (Fig. 7-34). In the first group cord 6 becomes the knot-bearing cord, and cords 5, 4, 3, 2, and 1 are knotted on it, in that order, in Diagonal Double Half Hitches. Cord 5 is used for a knot-bearing cord for the next row and cords 4, 3, 2, and 1 are knotted on it in succession. The next row is knotted over cord 4; then a row is tied over cord 3, and finally cord 1 is tied over cord 2. The same design is knotted in reverse with the second group of six cords. Then cords 1 and 2 may be tied in a Square Knot with the two remaining cords from the second group. The motifs in the photograph (Fig. 7-32) were knotted together, but the drawing (Fig. 7-34) omits this step. Two more triangular shapes are knotted with each group of six cords to complete one unit of the design.

E This band is the same as section A except that three rows of knots are tied instead of two.

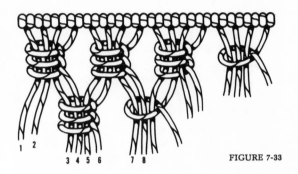

FIGURE 7-33

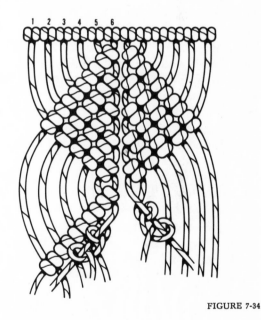

FIGURE 7-34

Combining colors in designs of macramé requires some very careful planning. If sharp color contrasts are used in an elaborate pattern, the piece will become very active and the design confused unless the colors are carefully arranged within the design.

The easiest way to combine colors is to knot several pieces, each in a color, and then assemble the parts. The collage shown in the frontispiece is a group of separate pieces assembled into a design. Beads add another dimension of color and texture.

Using more than one color of yarn in a knotted piece is much more difficult; however, attractive designs can be achieved with careful planning. Colors can be hidden in a knot-bearing cord, and thus they can be carried from one part of the design to another without being seen. Double Half Hitches knotted with a soft yarn will hide the color of the knot-bearing cord completely. In Fig. C-4 the gray cords in the yellow and gray piece appear and disappear to form the design. Can you tell how the cream-colored yarn moves from the center to the outside and back to the center in the tan, brown, and cream piece? Colors can also be hidden in the center cords of a flat or spiral sinnet, or in the center of some of the braids.

Double Half Hitches knotted continuously offer another opportunity to combine more than one color. Sometimes this technique of solid knotting is called "Cavandoli Work," "Knotted Tapestry," or "Gobelin Knotted Work." It is slow to knot because there are no open spaces, but it is easier to plan a design because it can be charted on graph paper. Fig. 7-35 is the plan for the solidly knotted piece shown in Fig. C-4. Each square on the graph paper represents one Double Half Hitch, and color changes are achieved by changing from Horizontal Double Half Hitch to Vertical Double Half Hitch. For instance, if you knot Horizontal Double Half Hitches with a white cord over a black knot-bearing cord, the knot is white. When you change to a Vertical Double Half Hitch, the black knot-bearing cord becomes the knotting cord and the white knotting cord becomes the knot-bearing cord; therefore the knot will be black (Figs. 7-36 and 7-37).

Four colors and Diagonal Double Half Hitches were used for knotting the mat in Figs. 7-38 and 7-39, and Fig. 7-40 shows the design on graph paper. The direction in which the knots are tied, which is indicated by the heavier lines on the graph paper, controls the color of the Diagonal Double Half Hitch in the same way that it does with the Horizontal and Vertical Double Half Hitch (Fig. 7-41).

More than one color is usually used in solid designs; however, one color can be quite handsome when the only pattern is the texture contrast caused by the change of direction of the knots (Fig. 7-42). Another way to create a pattern of texture contrast with Double Half Hitches is shown in Fig. 7-44. Knotting on the face of the piece, then turning the entire piece over and knotting on the reverse side, causes the change of surface.

This discussion of design and color in macramé has only scratched the surface. It is meant to lead you on to investigate and experiment. After you have mastered the knots and worked with the technique enough to understand the different ways the knots combine to form pattern, the next step is to plan your own designs.

Craftsmen today are using the knots in new ways to make designs that bear little resemblance to the early laces and fringes. As Figs. 7-44 through 7-47 show, new forms are used, and new materials are introduced into the knotting. Adding a third dimension gives new pattern and a play of light and shadow to the knotted work.

There are many avenues of approach for designing useful and beautiful articles of macramé. Some craftsmen sketch their ideas first (Figs. 7-48 and 7-49). Some experiment with materials and patterns by making samples; others work more freely, designing and improvising as they knot. Regardless of your approach, you will be working for harmony of texture, pattern, form, and color. No doubt you will have some successes, some failures, and some happy accidents — all of us do. However, the pure pleasure in a successful design you have created is more than worth the effort.

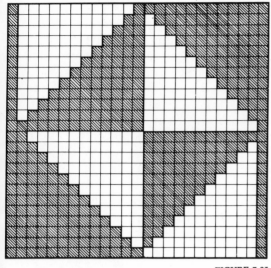

FIGURE 7-35

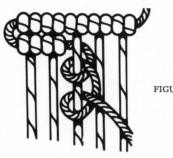

FIGURE 7-36

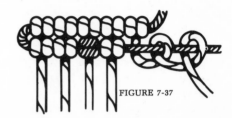

FIGURE 7-37

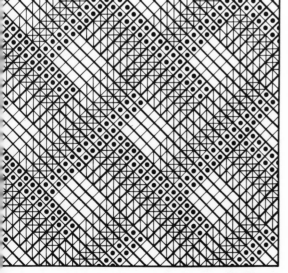

FIGURE 7-38

A mat knotted solidly with Diagonal Double Half Hitches in brown, rust, tan, and white cotton cord by Charles Frisbie. (Courtesy of Betsy Frisbie Ekvall)

FIGURE 7-39

The reverse side of the mat shown in Fig. 7-37.

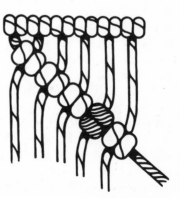

FIGURE 7-41

FIGURE 7-40

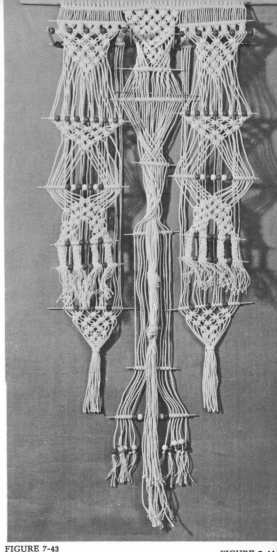

FIGURE 7-42

Yellow-tan linen upholsterers' twine was knotted in Diagonal Double Half Hitches in a pattern of textural changes.

A wall hanging that has been given a third dimension by using small flat pieces of wood like tongue depressors, small dowels, and beads as spacers. (Knotted by Milton Sonday)

Textural change produced by interchanging the face and reverse of the piece as the knotting progresses.

FIGURE 7-43

FIGURE 7-44

Three-dimensional hanging forms knotted by LeRoy Schwarcz. (Figs. 7-45 and 7-46 photographed by Albert C. Finn; Fig. 7-47 photographed by June Schwarcz)

FIGURE 7-45   FIGURE 7-46   FIGURE 7-47

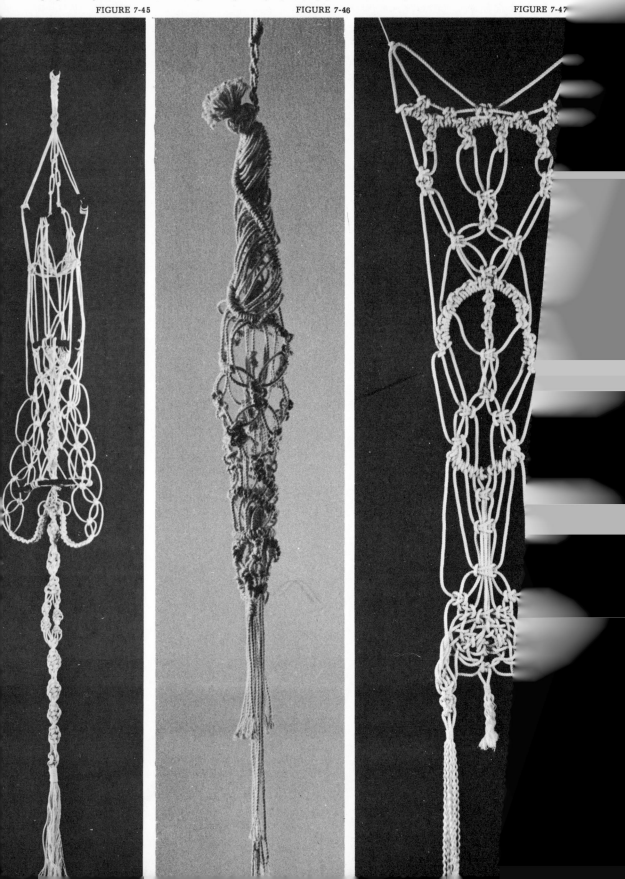

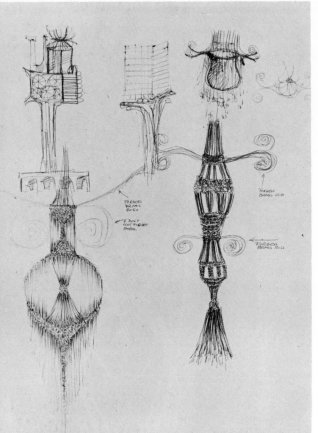

FIGURE 7-48

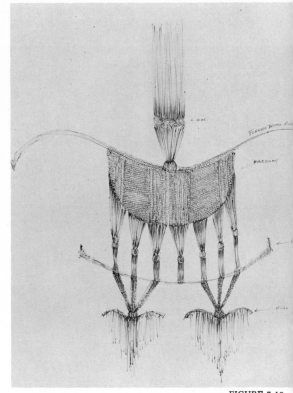

FIGURE 7-49

Pen and ink designs for macramé from the sketch pad of Robert Ebendorf.

FIGURE 7-50   (*opposite*)

This page from a sketchbook illustrates a few of the many variations that can be made with the diamond motif. The design at the top, left is a single diamond; at the top, right a row of diamonds is alternated with a different design. The piece at center, left has an over-all pattern of one diamond. The designs at center, right and bottom, left each use two diamonds in alternation. In the two samples at the bottom of the page, diamonds are placed within diamonds. (See Fig. 1-11 for still other variations on the diamond motif.)

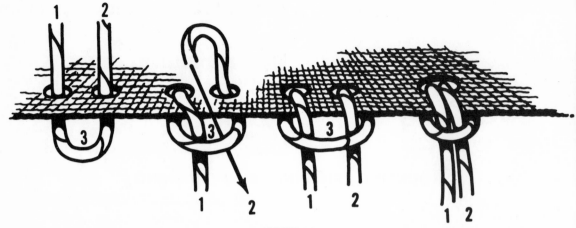

FIGURE 8-1

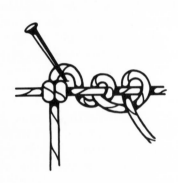

FIGURE 8-2

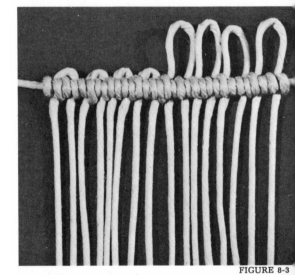

FIGURE 8-3

Cords mounted with the Double Half Hitch to make large and small picots.

Cords mounted with the Double Half Hitch and the Overhand Knot.

FIGURE 8-5

FIGURE 8-4

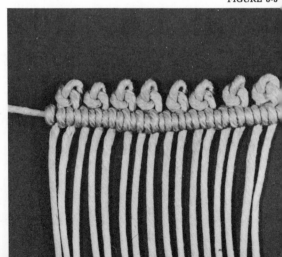

8

MOUNTING, SHAPING, AND FINISHING

A knotted piece is composed of many elements. Some of these — the yarn or cord, the knotting design, the pattern of the knotting — have been discussed in the foregoing pages. In this chapter we shall consider the way cords are mounted to begin the work, the shaping of the article, and the way the edges and the end of the knotting are finished. As you plan your piece, you should be sure all of these details work together to make a complete design and a functional article. A poor choice in any one will ruin the whole effect.

There are many ways to begin a piece. One way, the Reversed Double Half Hitch on a holding cord, has been explained before (see page 50). This mounting can be varied by placing the Reversed Double Half Hitch over a bar or a dowel instead of a holding cord. The garden hanging in Fig. 1-23 was started on a hardwood dowel.

Another mounting is shown in Fig. 2-11. A heavy piece of leather (or other material) is shaped and stitched, and holes are punched along the edge at measured intervals. The beginning cords are laced through the punched holes, as shown in Fig. 8-1. A cord is doubled, and each end is threaded upward through a hole from under the material and brought toward you. Then both ends come down over the edge of the material and through the loop formed by the doubled cord. Cords can also be attached in a single hole, as illustrated by the last cord on the right in Fig. 8-1. The holes must be spaced to hold the proper number of

cords per inch for the knotting, but not so close to each other or to the edge that the material will tear — so plan ahead! Experiment with some scraps of the material and a few cords to avoid mistakes later.

One of the simplest ways of mounting is to pin a doubled cord to your knotting surface and tie a Double Half Hitch over a holding cord with each end, as shown in Fig. 8-2. This mounting forms a row of *picots* at the beginning of the work, and the picots can be controlled so they are large or small, depending upon the effect you want (Fig. 8-3).

An Overhand Knot placed in the cord so it will be at the top of the picot changes the appearance of the mounted cords (Figs. 8-4 and 8-5). For instance, the knotting was begun at the upper edge of the bag in Fig. 8-6, and Overhand Knots were tied in each two cords before they were Half Hitched on the holding cord.

Double or triple picots form a scalloped edge (Fig. 8-7). The knotting cords are held in place with pins and knotted on the holding cord in order, working from either left to right or right to left (Fig. 8-8). Knotting over these picots with either the Half Hitch (Figs. 8-9, 8-10, and 8-11) or the Reversed Double Half Hitch (Figs. 8-12 and 8-13) forms an edge that is heavier and sturdier. Usually the center cords are mounted on the holding cord first, and Figs. 8-9, 8-10, and 8-12 show three cords attached with Reversed Double Half Hitches with the reverse side of the knot facing you. The last

FIGURE 8-6

Starting this bag with Overhand Knots tied before the cords are knotted on the holding cord gives the upper edge a finish that is compatible with the design of the bag as a whole. (Courtesy of Marietta M. Ward)

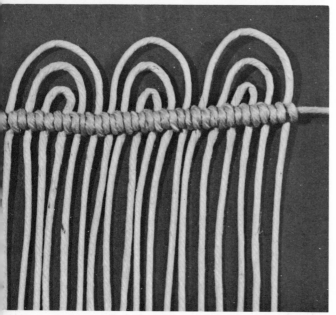

Cords mounted with the Double Half Hitch to make picots that form a scalloped edge.

FIGURE 8-7

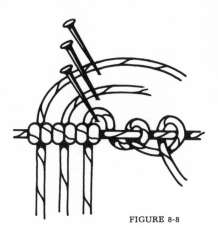

FIGURE 8-8

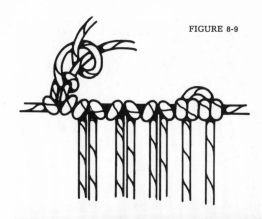

FIGURE 8-9

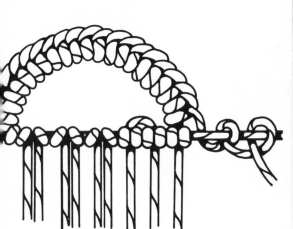

FIGURE 8-10

FIGURE 8-11

Cords mounted with Half Hitches knotted over the picots to form a scalloped edge.

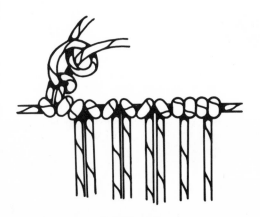

FIGURE 8-12

Cords mounted with Reversed Double Half Hitches knotted over the picots to form a scalloped edge.

FIGURE 8-13

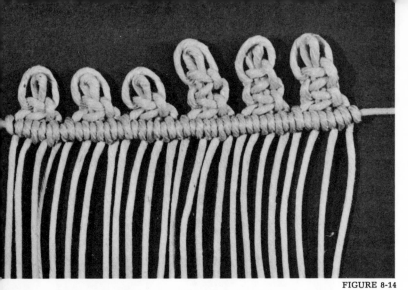

FIGURE 8-14

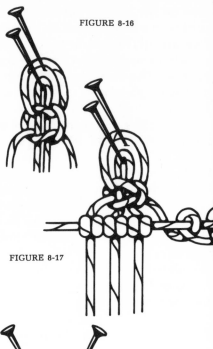

FIGURE 8-16

FIGURE 8-17

FIGURE 8-18

FIGURE 8-19

Square Knots are knotted as a heading before the cords are knotted on the holding cord with Double Half Hitches.

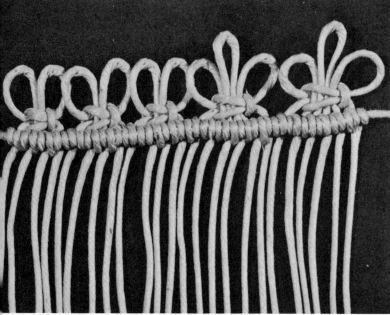

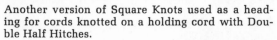

FIGURE 8-15

Another version of Square Knots used as a heading for cords knotted on a holding cord with Double Half Hitches.

Single and double chains are headings for cords knotted on a holding cord with Double Half Hitches.

FIGURE 8-20

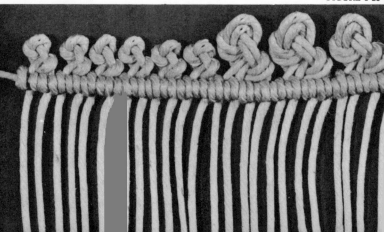

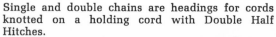

cord on the right is knotted on the holding cord with a Double Half Hitch. Both mountings are illustrated here to show you the possibilities; however, either method can be used. The center cords in Figs. 8-11 and 8-13 were placed on the holding cord with Reversed Double Half Hitches.

The cord that is used to make the scallop must be cut longer to allow for the extra knots. After this cord is attached to the holding cord with a Reversed Double Half Hitch, one end becomes the knot-bearing cord and the other end is used to knot over it. Large or small scallops can be made, depending upon the number of knots that are tied over the picots. When the scallop is completed, both the knot-bearing cord and the knotting cord are knotted on the holding cord with Double Half Hitches.

Square Knots combine in many ways to form a pattern at the beginning of a piece (Figs. 8-14 and 8-15). Pins hold the knotting cords in the proper position while you tie the Square Knots, and then the cords are knotted with the Double Half Hitch on the holding cord in the usual way. Figs. 8-16 through 8-19 show how the patterns in Figs. 8-14 and 8-15 are formed.

Short lengths of single or double chains, or both, can be used to mount cords in other patterns (Figs. 8-20 and 8-21).

Mountings can be made by working on a piece in one direction, then turning it and using the cords that are hanging for the body of the work. For instance, in Fig. 8-22 two knotting cords are doubled and attached to the working surface in the usual vertical position. The length of these cords, when doubled, should be three and a half to four times the *width* of the piece you are planning to make. The work is started with a small picot (Fig. 8-2), and the cords over which the Double Half Hitches are tied will become the knotting cords for the body of the piece. For this reason they should measure, when doubled, three and a half or four times the length of the piece you are planning to make. Fig. 8-22 illustrates the heading. The long knot-bearing cords are added horizontally to continue it, and the vertical cords are knotted over them with

Double Half Hitches until the piece is as long as the *width* of the planned piece. When the heading is completed, it is turned counterclockwise, so the right-hand edge in Fig. 8-22 becomes the top of the work, and the former knot-bearing cords become the knotting cords for the body of the piece. Fig. 8-23 shows a small part of a heading finished, turned, and ready to be knotted. It forms a solid band that is a firm beginning.

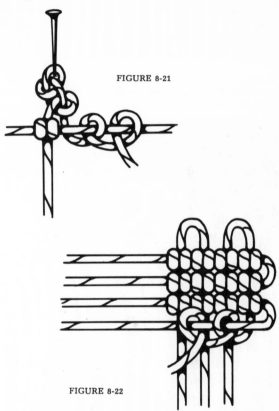

FIGURE 8-21

FIGURE 8-22

A turned mounting with Double Half Hitches.

FIGURE 8-23

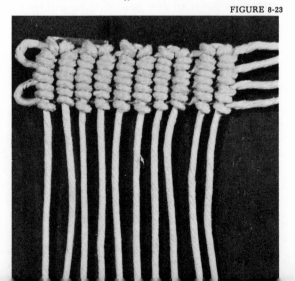

Another version of this heading is made by using one continuous cord to knot over, leaving loops at one edge large enough so you can attach knotting cords to them, as shown in Fig. 8-24. A heading for a pattern that requires spaced knotting cords is shown in Fig. 8-25.

As you can see from these examples, the beginning of your work can be decorative as well as functional. You may devise other ways to start that are better for the pieces you design. Any mounting is suitable if it works in the place it is used, and if it is compatible with the total design of the piece.

Many pieces that are knotted, such as place mats or envelope bags, are rectangular in shape, and some articles, such as the lamp shade in Fig. 1-11, are cylindrical. These forms are most frequently used, but it is also possible to shape a piece, making it larger by adding cords or smaller by subtracting them. Mountings and endings can be shaped also.

Perhaps the simplest shape is the point, and it can be knotted in several ways. If a holding cord is used, an uneven number of cords should be cut and mounted on it. Pin the cords to your working surface at the center knot, as shown in Fig. 8-26. The cords can be mounted with the Reversed Double Half Hitch (Figs. 8-27 and 8-28) or the Double Half Hitch (Figs. 8-29 and 8-30). Another pointed shape can be mounted by pinning the cords and knotting them, thus eliminating a holding cord (Figs. 8-31 and 8-32). The point is shaped when you tie the Square Knot in alternate arrangement, with one knot in the center, two below it, three in the next row, and so on.

These are small pointed shapes. If you use more cords and continue the mounting in the same way, a large pointed form will develop. The bag in Fig. 1-25 was started with a modified point and shaped by knotting over a pattern. The exact size and shape of the bag were planned and then drawn on the knotting surface. The bag was knotted in one flat piece (except for the small side pieces), starting at the bottom edge of the flap and knotting over the

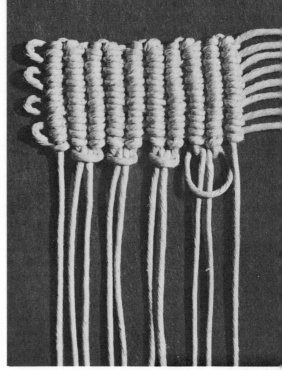

FIGURE 8-24
A turned mounting with Double Half Hitches and cords added with Reversed Double Half Hitches.

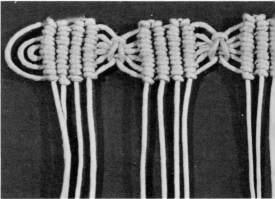

FIGURE 8-25
A turned mounting with Double Half Hitches and Square Knots.

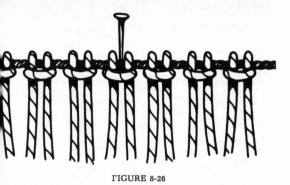

FIGURE 8-26

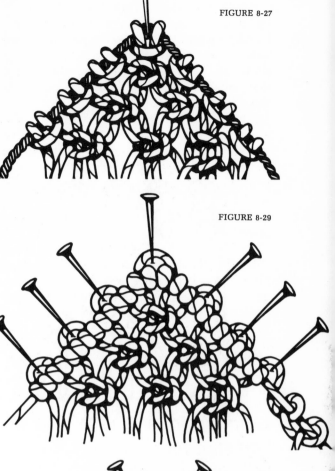

FIGURE 8-27

FIGURE 8-29

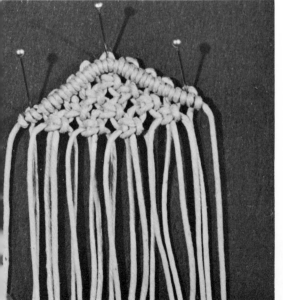

FIGURE 8-28

A point shaped with cords mounted on a holding cord with Reversed Double Half Hitches.

FIGURE 8-31

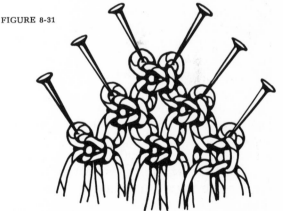

A point shaped with the Square Knot.

FIGURE 8-32

FIGURE 8-30

A point shaped with cords mounted on a holding cord with Double Half Hitches.

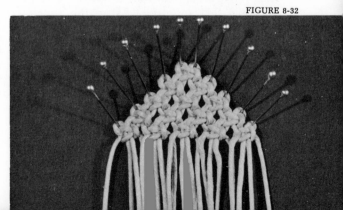

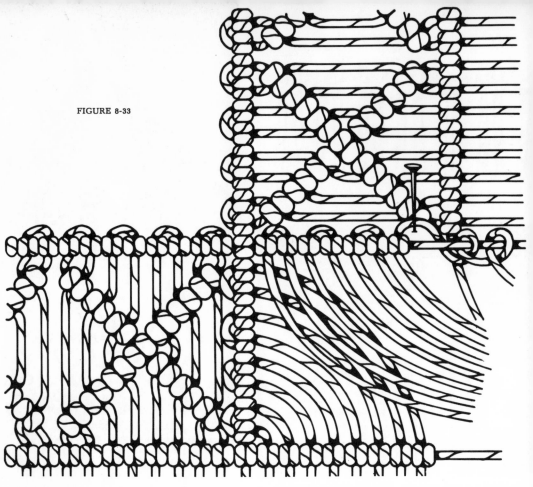

FIGURE 8-33

top, down the back, under the bottom, and up the front. The ending is under the flap. One of the reasons the knotting was done in this order was to secure and conceal the ends under the lining at a place where a little bulk would not detract from the appearance of the bag.

Any piece that becomes wider as the knotting progresses is shaped by adding cords. For instance, if you want to make a border for a rectangular piece and keep the knotting flat as it goes around each of the four corners, you might add cords as illustrated in Fig. 8-33.

Width is reduced in just the opposite way — cords that are not needed in the design are left inactive. After the piece is completed, they are knotted or worked into the back of the piece and trimmed. Fig. 8-34 shows how cords are dropped to begin the shaping of armholes. The cords that are not knotted when the armhole is shaped will be finished off, and a braid will be used as an edge trimming.

The bag in Fig. 8-35 is a fine example of shaping. The knotting was started in the solid area at the center of the bag and worked by turning the piece in much the same way as the mounting explained on page 109. The knotting cords were left hanging on each side of the work as the solid area was knotted (Fig. 8-36). Then the hanging cords were knotted and beads were included to form the more open pattern of chains around the solid center. Three rows of Double Half Hitches follow the open pattern area, and extra cords were added at the point, as shown in Fig. 8-37, to keep the work flat. The design of the bag continues with a row of short Square Knot sinnets, then another three rows of Double Half Hitches, another row of Square Knot sinnets, and a last three rows of Double Half Hitches. Cords were added at the point of each of the bands of Double Half Hitches.

Cords can be added by looping them into the work in many ways. The center cord in

FIGURE 8-34

A blouse shaped by knotting over a pattern drawn on the knotting surface. The knotter started at the lower edge of the garment, progressed toward the shoulders, and has begun to reduce the sides to conform with the armhole of the pattern. (Courtesy of Darlene Mapes)

An ingenious knotter started this bag at the solid area in the center and shaped it as he knotted. Tan wooden beads are used with the tan cotton cord. (Courtesy of Betsy Frisbie Ekvall)

FIGURE 8-35

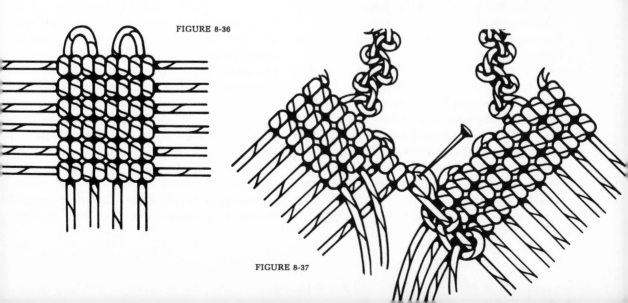

FIGURE 8-36

FIGURE 8-37

Fig. 8-38 is added with a Square Knot. An angle can be formed as shown in Fig. 8-39. Extra length is allowed for the knot-bearing cords on one edge of the piece; the work is turned, and the knotting is continued at a right angle. In this example the work is turned clockwise, and three of the former knot-bearing cords are used to knot the extension that forms the angle.

When elaborate trimmings were used in homes, doilies were made with circular shapes. Today we might use one for the crown of a pillbox hat. Circular shapes are started by placing some of your knotting cords on a holding cord. The ends of the holding cord are then overlapped, and the remaining cords are knotted over the two ends. When the required number have been placed on the knotting cord, the two ends are pulled to tighten the circle (Fig. 8-40). Cords are added as needed to keep the work from drawing in as the circle becomes larger (Fig. 8-41). Although the figure shows only one pin, it is advisable to keep the work pinned securely to a flat surface as the knotting progresses. The number of cords and the places in the knotting where they are added depend on the size of the cord you use and the pattern of the knotting.

Regardless of how carefully you plan and measure your cords, occasionally it will be necessary to replace a cord that is too short. There are several ways to do this, and the least noticeable way is the best. The way you choose will depend upon the design you are knotting.

With very thick cords it may be necessary to splice, but with smaller materials it is possible to add cords in the same way that you do when you are shaping a piece, as in Figs. 8-33, 8-37, and 8-38. Or, if you are knotting Double Half Hitches, you can knot over two cords for a short distance, then drop the short cord and continue to knot over the added cord (Fig. 8-42). The ends are clipped when the work is finished. Another place in knotting where it is possible to add a cord is in the core of a sinnet or braid.

Most often it seems that cords run out in the most inconvenient place, such as the middle of a pattern where there is no place to hide the ends. Fig. 8-43 shows you how to replace a cord in such a situation. The short end 1 is dropped, and the new cord 2 is pinned to the knotting surface and brought into the knotting to replace the short cord. After the piece is finished, the end of the short cord and the end of the new cord are tied on the reverse side of the material, or they are worked into the reverse of the knotting with a needle.

Finishing the edges and the end of a piece is important to the appearance of the knotting. If you pin the sides of your knotting to the working surface as you knot and do not leave any long loops or ends, the edges should be presentable when the piece is finished. It is advisable to have some lines on the working surface as guides for pinning the knotting so it is straight and square.

Sometimes a pattern will continue to the edge of a piece; at other times a border is required. In the long, narrow wall hanging in Fig. 8-44, some of the patterns are knotted to the edge, while others are framed with vertical lines of Square Knots that are knotted like the sinnet in Fig. 5-6. Any one of the braids in Figs. 6-25 or 6-33, the single chain in Fig. 6-20, or the double chain in Fig. 6-18 could be used in the same way. The Vertical Double Half Hitch is used for the borders in the last section of the sampler in Chapter Five (see Fig. 5-46) and for the borders and dividers in the wall hanging in Fig. 7-18. The edges of the evening bag in Fig. 1-25 were finished with Vertical, Horizontal — and, I suppose, the knots on the flap should be called Diagonal — Double Half Hitches. Actually, what they are called is not important. The important point is that Double Half Hitches can be knotted either vertically, horizontally, diagonally, or in a circle, if necessary, and they will form an attractive, continuous pattern as an edge.

If you are knotting a project in several pieces to be assembled after they are finished, many of the braids make functional

FIGURE 8-38　　　　　　　　　FIGURE 8-39　　　　　　　　　FIGURE 8-40

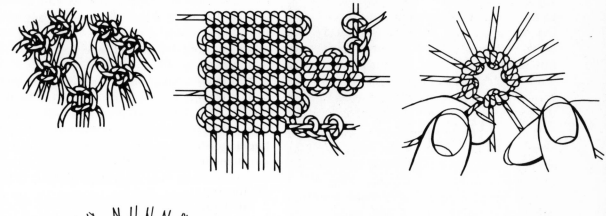

FIGURE 8-41

FIGURE 8-42

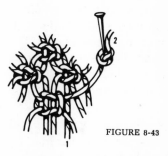

FIGURE 8-43

edges. When a braid with picots or loops on its edge is incorporated in a border design, the loops are very convenient for lacing two edges together (Fig. 8-45). Loops on the edges can also be knotted together with Square Knots (Figs. 8-46 and 8-47).

The easiest solution for finishing the end of a piece is a simple fringe. After you have knotted the last knot, all you need to do is trim the fringe, and you are finished. A more sturdy fringe can be made by twisting each of two groups of cords in a clockwise direction and then combining the two groups by twisting them together in a counterclockwise direction. An Overhand Knot at the end will keep them from untwisting (Figs. 8-48 and 8-49).

Unfortunately, not all pieces can be finished with a fringe. Fringes tend to wear

out or become ragged after they have been washed a few times, and they are not suitable to the function or the design of some pieces. If a solid end is needed, there are at least three ways to finish a piece.

For one finish, two rows of Double Half Hitches are knotted. Then a crochet hook is used to pull the ends back through the knotting between the rows, one cord in each opening (Fig. 8-50). The cords are then knotted on the reverse side (Fig. 8-51) and clipped. Depending upon the way the knotted piece is to be used, sometimes a drop of glue is added to each knot to make it more secure.

Another finish that forms a solid end is a facing. A piece of tape is stitched by machine to the ends on the face, or right side of the piece, at the very edge of the knot-

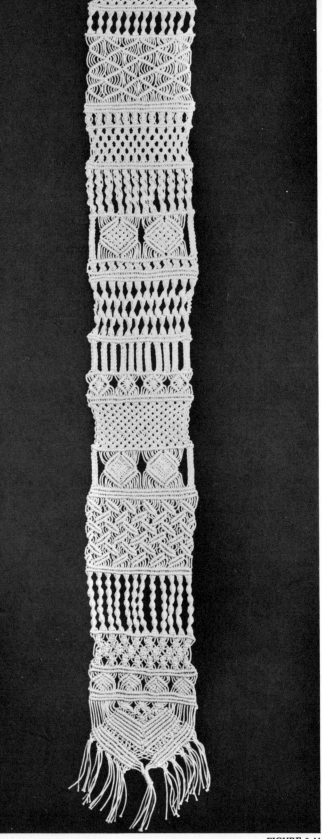

FIGURE 8-44

Yellow-tan upholsterers' cord was used to knot a variety of patterns in this wall hanging.

ting (Fig. 8-52). The ends of the cords are trimmed, and the tape is turned and hand-stitched to the back of the piece, covering the clipped ends (Fig. 8-53). The machine stitching holds the ends, and the finish is neat and secure.

The third finish that forms a solid end is made with a needle or a crochet hook. The door mat in Figs. 8-54 and 8-55 is finished this way, and a special tool is used because of the size of the material. Each end is threaded back through the knotting on the reverse side and then clipped (Fig. 8-56). Glue may also be applied to these cords after the edge is finished if the piece is to receive hard wear (Fig. 8-57).

It is possible to finish a piece using a bar or dowel, so the end has the same appearance as a mounting made with Reversed Double Half Hitches over a dowel. The wall hangings in Figs. 1-18 and 1-19 are finished this way. When the knotting is completed, it is placed face down, and the dowel is laid across the cords just below the last row of knotting. As illustrated in Fig. 8-58, these cords are knotted together in groups of two. The right-hand cord is bent over the bar and passed under the two cords from right to left between the dowel and the last row of knotting. The left-hand cord is bent over the dowel and passed under the same two cords from left to right. The two ends are then knotted together in a Square Knot over the two cords and clipped.

Sometimes, rather than concealing the ends, you can use them as a part of the design. The problem of finishing was solved in an interesting way in the bag in Fig. 8-59. The little tassel created by the ends is decorative, and the graduated size of the last row of knots covering the ends enhances the total design of the bag.

As you can see, there are many ways to finish the edges and the end of knotting, and each project you plan will have some conditions that must be satisfied. One of the finishes mentioned here may satisfy those conditions, or you may have to design a different edge. Maybe you will invent one that has never been used before!

FIGURE 8-45   FIGURE 8-46   FIGURE 8-47

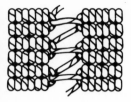

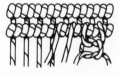

FIGURE 8-50   FIGURE 8-51

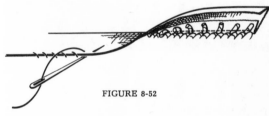

FIGURE 8-48

FIGURE 8-49

FIGURE 8-52

A door mat knotted in Square Knots with single strands of rope unwound from a three-strand rope. The tool seen here was devised to work the ends back into the reverse side to finish the mat. (Courtesy of the State of Washington, Department of Labor and Industries, Dr. H. T. Buckner Rehabilitation Center for Injured Workers)

A mat finished by facing with tape.

FIGURE 8-53   FIGURE 8-54

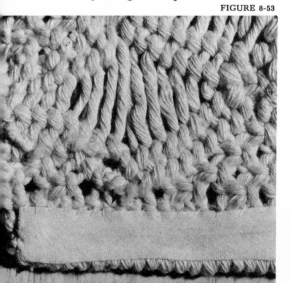

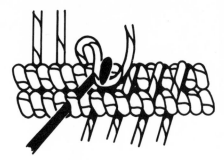

FIGURE 8-55

FIGURE 8-56

A corner of the face of the finished door mat. At bottom is the edge that is being finished in Fig. 8-54. This kind of mat is one of the projects suggested to patients by occupational therapists. (Courtesy of the State of Washington, Department of Labor and Industries, Dr. H. T. Buckner Rehabilitation Center for Injured Workers)

Section of a knotted belt that was finished by pulling the ends through loops on the underside of the knotting, trimming them, and applying glue to hold them. The face of this belt is shown in Fig. 1-24.

FIGURE 8-57

FIGURE 8-58

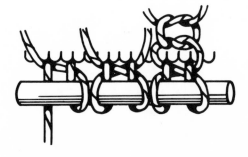

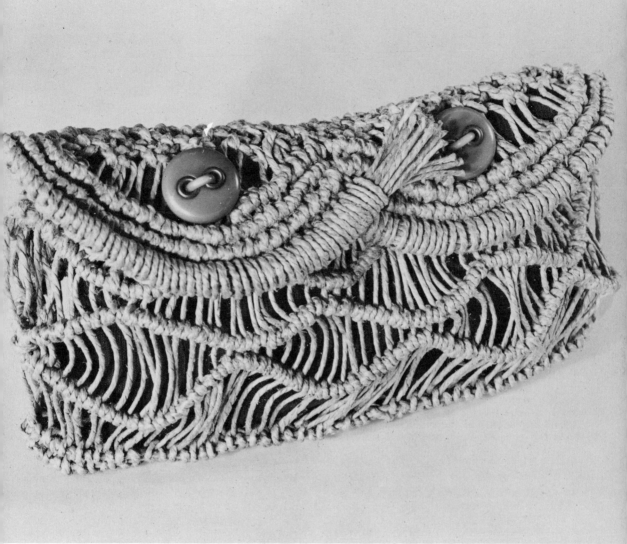

FIGURE 8-59

Tan jute wrapping twine was knotted into this attractive envelope bag by Harriet Marshall.

FIGURE 9-1

A white jute place mat.

9

PLANNING A KNOTTED PROJECT

In the preceding chapters you have seen many examples of articles that can be made with macramé, learned about the materials and tools to use, and knotted small pieces to learn the knots. You have seen how the knots combine to form pattern and, finally, you have learned some of the ways to mount, shape, and finish a project. These chapters should be used for reference as you plan your knotted projects.

This last chapter will lead you, step-by-step, through the planning, preparation, and knotting of a project. Of course, any piece you decide to make will have problems to solve that are unique to that piece, but this will give you a general outline to follow.

A rectangular piece that can be used for a place mat or made into an envelope bag has been selected for the project. It has an open pattern of Square Knots and Diagonal Double Half Hitches that can be knotted in a few evenings, and both the mat and the bag are useful and attractive (Figs. 9-1 and 9-2).

Jute-tone, a jute yarn that is available at weavers' supply houses, is the material selected, because it makes a heavy, serviceable mat that is inexpensive. The yarn is sold in tubes, and four tubes are needed for this project. A sample about four inches square should be knotted in the pattern to be used (Fig. 9-3). This is used as a gauge to determine the number of cords per inch in the mat. Placing a ruler at the top of the sample, you will find six cords per inch. This means that three cords per inch must be doubled and placed on the holding cord.

Next, the total number of cords needed must be calculated. The finished mat will measure approximately 13 by 18 inches, and it is started by mounting a sufficient number of cords for the width and then knotted until it is 18 inches long. If you multiply six cords per inch by 13 inches, you find that seventy-eight cords should be cut. However, you must also consider the number of cords that are needed to make the pattern, so a little more arithmetic is necessary. If you use four cords to make lines of Diagonal Double Half Hitches (these form the diamonds in the design), separate each group of four by sixteen cords, and allow a group of eight cords at each side, the total is eighty cords (Fig. 9-4). The pattern balances if you add two cords to the seventy-eight needed for the 13-inch width. So you want eighty cords in all — or forty cords doubled and mounted on the holding cord.

Now you must decide what length to measure the cords. As you have seen in Chapter Four, the cords should be measured three and a half or four times the length of the finished article; however, you should remember, a thick cord takes up more in length. The length of the mat, 18 inches, multiplied by four equals 72 inches. Since the jute is a heavy cord, you should add another yard, making each cord 108 inches long. (When the mat is completed, you will note that the cords remaining in the center are longer than those left at the sides. The extra Square Knots tied along the sides take up the additional length.) C-clamps are placed 108 inches apart, and eighty cords are measured on them (Fig. 4-1).

These long cords are mounted with Reversed Double Half Hitches on a holding cord that should be 48 inches long. Fig. 9-5 shows an easy method for mounting them. When all of the cords are measured the proper length, tie a string around them about 12 inches from one of the C-clamps. Here are the doubled ends that will be mounted on the holding cord, so lift them off the C-clamp, and do not cut them. Cut the other ends to remove them from the clamp. The doubled, uncut ends, held together by the cord that was tied around them, are then placed on the holding cord.

Now you are ready to mount your material on a knotting board. The board should be prepared by marking on it a rectangle 13 by 18 inches, the size of the finished piece (Fig. 9-6). Pin your holding cord at the top of the rectangle, and shorten your knotting cords by winding them into bobbins (see Figs. 4-11 and 4-12). A pin is placed at the right-hand edge of the work; the holding cord is turned and used as a knot-bearing cord for a row of Horizontal Double Half Hitches. It is then turned around another pin at the left-hand edge and used again as the knot-bearing cord for a second row of Horizontal Double Half Hitches. (This knot-bearing cord is not used further in the pattern, so it is left hanging until the mat is completed. Then it is worked into the back of the piece with a needle, and the end is clipped.)

This brings you to the beginning of the Square Knots and Diagonal Double Half Hitches that form the pattern. Separate your cords into groups (Fig. 9-7) according to the count in Fig. 9-4.

Starting at the right side as illustrated in Fig. 9-8, the first eight cords are tied in two Square Knots. Then cords 1 and 2 are left inactive, and cords 3, 4, 5, and 6 are tied in a Square Knot below and in alternate arrangement to the first two knots. Continuing the alternate arrangement, a third Square Knot is tied with cords 1, 2, 3, and 4 just below and to the right of the last knot.

The next four cords to the left (cords 9, 10, 11, and 12) are used to start the diagonal lines. Cord 11 becomes the knot-bearing cord, and cords 10, 9, 8, 7, 6, 5, 4, 3, 2, and 1 are knotted on it, in that order, with Diagonal Double Half Hitches. This and the following steps are shown in Fig. 9-9.

Cord 10, which you have just knotted on cord 11, will become the knot-bearing cord for the diagonal that goes from right to left. Cord 12, which will become the knot-bearer for the second diagonal that goes from left to right, is knotted on cord 10 with a Diagonal Double Half Hitch. Cords 10 and 12 are left for the moment.

Next, cords 13 through 28 are knotted to make a row of four Square Knots. Then three Square Knots are tied in alternate arrangement in a second row; two Square Knots form the third row, and one Square Knot finishes the point formed by these knots. Now the diagonal that was started by knotting cord 12 on cord 10 is continued by knotting cords 13 through 20 on cord 10 with Diagonal Double Half Hitches.

As you have seen in the photograph of the finished piece (Fig. 9-1), there are two rows of Diagonal Double Half Hitches for each of the diagonal lines, so now the second rows must be added (Figs. 9-9 and 9-10). Cord 12 becomes the knot-bearer for the second diagonal row parallel to the row knotted over cord 11, and all the cords that were knotted on cord 11 are knotted on cord 12 in the same order. Cord 9 is the knot-bearer for the row parallel to cord 10, and the same cords knotted on cord 10 are knotted on it.

Cords 29, 30, 31, and 32 are tied in exactly the same way as cords 9, 10, 11, and 12, and the triangles of Square Knots with borders of Diagonal Double Half Hitches are repeated across the width of the mat, ending with a half triangle, exactly like the beginning of the pattern.

A Square Knot is tied at the intersection of the diagonals (Fig. 9-11), and then the diagonals are continued. At the edges of the mat the cords are turned to change the direction of the diagonal. At the right edge cord 12 is looped around cord 11 and a pin is inserted in the loop to hold it in place

FIGURE 9-2

The knotted piece in Fig. 9-1 folded to make an envelope bag.

FIGURE 9-3

A sample is knotted as a gauge to determine how many cords per inch are needed to make the mat in Fig. 9-1.

FIGURE 9-5

An easy way to handle long cords when they are being mounted on a holding cord.

The cords are divided into groups for the pattern and marked with pins.

FIGURE 9-7

FIGURE 9-6

A paper pattern has been cut and pinned to this knotting surface.

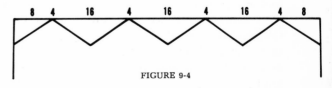

FIGURE 9-4

123

FIGURE 9-8

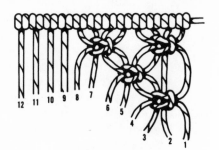

FIGURE 9-9

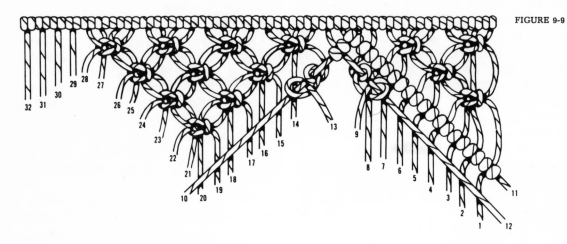

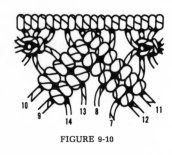

FIGURE 9-10

FIGURE 9-11

FIGURE 9-12

(Fig. 9-12). Cords 1, 2, 3, 4, 5, 6, 7, and 8 are knotted on cord 12, then on cord 11. The same procedure is followed at the left edge of the mat except that it is worked from left to right.

The lower part of each diamond is completed with two rows of Diagonal Double Half Hitches, knotting the cords in sequence as they come from the upper part of the diamond. Square Knots are knotted in alternate arrangement in the small triangles at the edges of the piece.

The pattern is continued until the piece is 18 inches long, or as near to 18 inches as possible with a completed pattern of diamonds. Finish the pattern of the mat to match the top by knotting Square Knots in the triangular areas, and then knot three rows of Horizontal Double Half Hitches. The end of the mat is finished with a facing (see Figs. 8-52 and 8-53).

If you wish to make the piece into an envelope bag, it should be folded in thirds so it measures about 6 by 13 inches. Either sew or knot the sides together (see Figs. 8-46 and 8-47) and line the purse.

If you review the directions for this project, you will see that it was planned in the following order:

1. Decide what to make.
2. Choose the pattern and material. (You may knot samples of several materials and patterns before you find the best combination for your project. When you have made your choice, the sample can be used as the gauge to calculate the amount of material you will need and the number and length of the cords to be cut.)
3. Measure, cut, and mount the yarns on a working surface.
4. Knot the article.
5. Finish the article carefully.

If you are reluctant to design your own projects instead of working from specific directions someone else has written, it may help you to follow this general outline. You may follow it exactly for the first few pieces you make or rearrange the steps — for instance, you may find a material or a pattern that inspires you before you decide what you want to make.

This is only one of many approaches to designing a piece in macramé. Sometimes a project is planned to the last detail before it is started; at other times it is possible to work more freely, composing as you knot. Regardless of how you work, take joy in the knotting itself — to create something beautiful from a ball of string or a cone of yarn should bring you pleasure, from the birth of the idea to the completion of the article.

LIST OF SUPPLIERS

Frederick J. Fawcett, Inc.
129 South Street
Boston, Massachusetts 02111
A weavers' supply house that is a good source for linen cords and yarns.

P. C. Herwig Company
264 Clinton Street
Brooklyn, New York 11201
A square-knotters' supply house that has cotton, rayon, and nylon yarns especially selected for knotting. They can supply books, belt buckles, and other items.

Magnolia Weaving
2635 29th West
Seattle, Washington 98199
A weavers' supply house that has cotton, wool, jute, and some man-made yarns for knotting.

Mrs. Lyle B. Robinson
1019 N. E. 62nd
Seattle, Washington 98115
A weavers' supply house that carries marine cords and lines and upholsterers' twines especially selected for knotting.

Troy Yarn and Textile Company
Pawtucket, Rhode Island 02860
A weavers' supply house that is an excellent source for wool rug yarns.

William and Company
Box 318 Madison Square Station
New York, New York 10010
A weavers' supply house that specializes in linen yarns, cords, and twines that are excellent for knotting.

The Yarn Depot
545 Sutter Street
San Francisco, California 94102
A weavers' supply house that carries cotton, jute, and wool yarns that are good knotting yarns and come in exciting colors.

BIBLIOGRAPHY

Anchor Manual of Needlework (2nd ed.). London, England: B. T. Batsford Ltd., 1966.

Ashley, Clifford W. *The Ashley Book of Knots*. Garden City, New York: Doubleday and Company, 1944.

Birrell, Verla. *The Textile Arts*. New York: Harper and Brothers, 1959.

Bocher, Emmanuel. *Manuel Des Travaux à L'Aiguille*, V. Paris: E. Rahir, 1919.

Brandt-Moller, F. and Kaj Lund. *Knyttebogen*. Kobenhavn, Denmark: Bogens Forlag, Jarl Borgen, no date.

De Dillmont, Th. *Encyclopedia of Needlework*. Alsace, France: Mulhouse, no date.

———. *Le Macramé*. Alsace, France: Mulhouse, no date.

Graumont, Raoul and Elmer Wenstrom. *Square Knot Handicraft Guide*. Cambridge, Maryland: Cornell Maritime Press, 1949.

Graumont, Raoul and John Hensel. *Encyclopedia of Knots and Fancy Rope Work*. Cambridge, Maryland: Cornell Maritime Press, 1943.

———. *Square Knot, Tatting, Fringe and Needlework*. Cambridge, Maryland: Cornell Maritime Press, 1943.

P. C. Herwig Company. *Square Knot Booklet #1, Square Knot Booklet #2, Square Knot Booklet #3*. New York: P. C. Herwig Company, no date.

Palliser, Mrs. Bury. *History of Lace*. London: Sampson Low, Marston and Company, 1910.

Rouillion, Marjorie Cordley. "Macramé in Mitla," *Craft Horizons*, November/December 1953.

Sylvia's Book of Macramé Lace. [ca.1882-1885.]

Whiting, Gertrude. *Tools and Toys of Stitchery*. New York: Columbia University Press, 1928.

GLOSSARY AND INDEX OF KNOTS

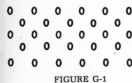

FIGURE G-1

Alternate Arrangement, G-1 — An over-all pattern in which rows of knots or motifs form diagonal as well as horizontal lines.

Diagonal Double Half Hitch — A Double Half Hitch that is tied over a diagonal knot-bearing cord (page 61).

Double Chain — Four cords separated into two pairs of two strands each and tied alternately with Half Hitches (page 73).

Double Half Hitch — A cord looped two times around one or more cords (page 59).

Filler Cords

FIGURE G-2

Filler Cords, G-2 — The two center cords of the Square Knot.

Flat or Square Knot Sinnet — Square Knots tied repeatedly with four cords (page 56).

Half Hitch — A cord looped around one or more cords.

Half Knot — Half of a Square Knot (page 55).

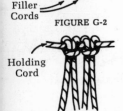

Holding Cord

FIGURE G-3

Holding Cord, G-3 — Cord over which other cords are knotted, usually at the beginning of the work.

Horizontal Double Half Hitch — A Double Half Hitch that is tied over a horizontal knot-bearing cord (page 59).

Josephine Knot ("Carrick Bend") — Two cords intertwined to form an oval-shaped knot (page 71).

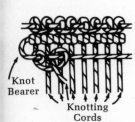

Knot Bearer

Knotting Cords

FIGURE G-4

Knot-Bearer or Knot-Bearing Cord, G-4 — The cord over which the knots are tied.

Knotting Cord — The cord with which the knots are tied.

Overhand Knot — A looped knot that can be tied with one or more cords (page 69).

Picot — A loop of cord projecting beyond the work (page 105).

Reversed Double Half Hitch — A cord looped two times around one or more cords, the second loop in the direction opposite to the first loop (page 50 and page 75).

FIGURE G-5

Single Chain — Two cords tied alternately with Half Hitches (page 73).

Sinnet — See: Flat; Spiral.

Spiral Sinnet — Half Knots tied repeatedly with four cords (page 55).

Square Knot G-5 — A knot usually composed of two knotting cords tied over two filler cords. The number of cords employed can be varied (page 56).

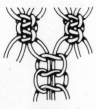

FIGURE G-6

Triple Knot, G-6 — A knot that is composed of a Square Knot plus a Half Knot (page 83).

Vertical Double Half Hitch — A Double Half Hitch that is tied over a vertical knot-bearing cord (page 62).